100 THINGS
MAPLE LEAFS FANS
SHOULD KNOW & DO
BEFORE THEY DIE

100 THINGS
MAPLE LEAFS FANS
SHOULD KNOW & DO
BEFORE THEY DIE

Mike Leonetti and Paul Patskou

TRIUMPH
BOOKS

Library of Congress Cataloging-in-Publication Data available upon request.

This book is available in quantity at special discounts for your group or organization. For further information, contact:
Triumph Books LLC
814 North Franklin Street
Chicago, Illinois 60610
(312) 337-0747
www.triumphbooks.com

Printed in U.S.A.
ISBN: 978-1-62937-837-4
Design by Patricia Frey
Photos courtesy of the author unless otherwise indicated.

This book is dedicated to all the loyal fans of the Toronto Maple Leafs. Young or old, we all share the same passion for this special hockey team that is near and dear to our hearts. Our bond with the Maple Leafs is something that will never change.

Contents

Introductions

The earliest hockey memory I have is of the magical 1958–59 season when the Leafs made the playoffs on the last night by one point. On Saturday nights, we all watched *Hockey Night In Canada* starting at 9:00 PM, and the game was joined in progress halfway through the second period. Foster Hewitt would give his postgame summary, with Toronto always "in the cellar." But that's when I fell in love with the underdog Leafs. I treasured my hockey cards from that year (five-cent packs—four cards and a gum). My Bob Nevin card still has the gum imprint on it!

The first Leaf game I went to was on February 22, 1964, and that was the night of the famous trade that brought Andy Bathgate to the Leafs. That was thrilling.

I also saw the Leafs win four Stanley Cups in the '60s—and, of course, none since.

My co-author in the first edition of this book, Mike Leonetti, sadly passed away in 2016 and there cannot be a more devoted Leaf fan than Mike was. This book is dedicated to his memory.

I hope you enjoy the revised and updated version of our book.

—Paul Patskou
March 2020

The first hockey season I can recall was the 1963–64 National Hockey League campaign, which featured six teams competing for the Stanley Cup. I turned six that year and my favourite team, the Toronto Maple Leafs, were favoured to repeat as Stanley Cup champions for the third year in a row. The '63–'64 Maple Leafs was a club that featured many stars and future Hall of Fame players like

Tim Horton, Johnny Bower, Allan Stanley, Frank Mahovlich, Red Kelly, Bob Pulford, Dave Keon, and captain George Armstrong. I followed their exploits on both television and radio and loved their home sweater with the rich blue colour base and the 35-point white Maple Leaf as the logo. The team played in Maple Leaf Gardens in those days and for most boys growing up in Toronto at that time, it was our "field of dreams." The Leafs only managed a third-place finish that year but in the playoffs, they rose to the occasion and won two seven-game series to capture their third straight title. As captain George Armstrong said after it was all over, "We never lost the last game." The most memorable games that year came in the postseason. Keon scored three goals right in Montreal to get the Leafs back to the Stanley Cup final and then the Toronto side won both Games 6 (on Bobby Baun's overtime goal) and 7 against the Detroit Red Wings (a 4–0 win at the Gardens) to hold the crown. Needless to say, it was a great time to be a Maple Leaf fan in the great city of Toronto and the team made everyone proud!

Three years later the Leafs once again won the Stanley Cup when they surprised the hockey world by beating Montreal in the final. Actually, they had shocked the first-place Chicago Black Hawks in the semi-final that year and then behind the superlative goaltending of Terry Sawchuk and Johnny Bower, they edged the mighty Canadiens in six games. The Leafs got many great performances in the '67 postseason and none was better than Dave Keon (my hero) who was awarded the Conn Smythe Trophy as the best player in the playoffs. The '67 triumph was the Leafs' fourth of the decade and the city seemed somewhat blasé about the win since it had become commonplace to see the Leafs hold a parade on Bay Street. If we Leaf fans had only known what was in store for us!

Since those great days of the 1960s the Leafs have experienced little success on the ice. No championships since '67 and not even an appearance in the Stanley Cup final. Sure, there have been many great players to wear the sweater since the last title—including

Darryl Sittler, Lanny McDonald, Borje Salming, Doug Gilmour, Wendel Clark, and Mats Sundin—but none have been able, despite their best efforts, to take the Leafs to a Stanley Cup victory. The best the Leafs have managed is five appearances among the final four teams competing for the Cup and that remains the same now.

The Leafs are a very successful business with an incredibly loyal fan base that brings millions of dollars to the organization year after year. Owners have changed, a new arena was built, coaches and managers have come and gone, the sweater has changed, but the lack of success on the ice continues unabated while the business side of the operation becomes more valuable as each year passes. It has become quite the conundrum and the organization must bear the burden of trying to get the team back to its glorious past while trying to still be the most profitable team in the entire NHL. Leaf fans can only hope that fresh faces and approaches from people like Brendan Shanahan can find the right balance to keep the Leafs successful in every way, but it will not be an easy task.

This book is for Maple Leafs fans who enjoy rooting for the blue and white no matter what situation is at hand. These fans are a resilient lot with a great deal of patience for their local heroes. Covered in these pages are a wide variety of issues, controversies, trivia, and fun facts to give the reader something different on each page. Some points will bring large agreement and some might cause some consternation but Leaf fans can be assured of some thought-provoking fun, facts, and figures.

Toronto's National Hockey League franchise celebrated its 100th anniversary as a member of the circuit that began play to start the 1917–18 season. This book will focus on more current events and the more recent past than on ancient history (which has been chronicled many times already). We hope this will make for a more dynamic read and include a younger generation of Maple Leafs fans.

The city of Toronto (a cosmopolitan place with a diversity of cultures) and surrounding area deserves a great hockey team and the inhabitants of this part of the world are ready to embrace a new group of champions like never before (see the reaction of Maple Leafs fans when the team made the playoffs in 2013). We cannot be sure when a Stanley Cup championship is going to happen for the Maple Leafs but we can have some fun looking back while we hope the future brings back the glory days we were once accustomed to in Toronto—just like when I was a young fan. Enjoy!

—Mike Leonetti
July 2014

1The Maple Leafs' Top Problem

For years now, many in the Toronto media and sports analysts in general across Canada (and even in the United States) blame the Maple Leaf fans who fill the newly named Scotiabank Arena game after game despite years of mediocre play by their favourite team. It used to be written that the Leafs had sold out every game since 1946 and although that was never exactly the case (especially when the team was a wretched organization in the 1980s), it is true that Leaf fans have stayed a devoted and caring group to the team wearing blue and white. The argument goes that empty seats would spur management to do more to make the Maple Leafs a winning club. Seven years ago, the *Toronto Sun* newspaper listed the top reasons why the Leafs were constantly failing and at the top of the list were Leaf fans who buy tickets and go to the games year in and year out. The reality is that nothing could be further from the truth.

Any sports team wants and needs to sell tickets to survive wherever they are located. Loyal Leaf fans have taken away the main worry of any sports team with consistent sellouts (although not quite every seat) and that should free up management to concentrate on what they need to do to make the team a winner. Money is not a problem for the Maple Leafs as fans and corporations are quite willing to pay top dollar (if not exorbitant rates) to see their local heroes play every winter. As a result, the Leafs are a wealthy team and should use their resources wisely to build the best management group and team possible.

If Scotiabank Arena (and before that the Air Canada Centre and Maple Leaf Gardens) was half empty would it really make a difference? It might cause alarm but would the management of the

Maple Leafs fans are always optimistic about their team. (Harold Barkley Archives)

team now decide they should make good trades and sign top free agents as a result? The answer is that the people who have run the Leafs since 1967 have all tried to make the team better but with mixed or outright bad results. It's not that they did not try—they were just not competent enough to get the job done properly. Under the ownership of Harold Ballard for instance it would not have made an ounce of difference if the Gardens was completely devoid of fans. Ballard really had no clue how to put a winning team together, but he loved being the boss of the Maple Leafs and all that went with that position.

The list of inadequate general managers and coaches who have run the Leafs since '67 (when Toronto last won a Stanley Cup) is far too long. One poor hire after another only gave Leaf supporters more grief as the beloved team sank lower in the standings most years. Ballard's passing brought some relief (ever so briefly) to long-suffering Leaf fans but only after a protracted battle for control of the team which was played out in board rooms and court rooms. Sure, many things did improve under new ownership but never enough to make the Leafs a championship team or even a consistent contender.

Fans are helpless to solve these issues but to blame them is ridiculous and an insult. In the modern era of the game, fans, including loyal Leafs supporters, have become less relevant in any event considering that so much money is coming to the team in the form of broadcasting revenues mostly from regular television and cable contracts. The league-wide salary cap instituted by NHL commissioner Gary Bettman and the owners has also taken away an advantage Toronto might have continued to enjoy by outspending others, but this had nothing to do with Leaf fans. Toronto fans deserve to be rewarded with a winning product—not chastised for being loyal to their favourite team. Poor ownership and management are where the finger of blame should be pointed at for the Leafs' largely inept record since '67. No Toronto fan should feel that shame. Fans should always be respected because it is their undying passion that not only keeps the great game of hockey alive and well, but also gives life to the premier franchise of the NHL.

2 Hockey Night in Canada

The question of why the Maple Leafs are so popular despite their unenviable record since 1967 is one that is asked over and over again, but there is really only one answer and that is *Hockey Night in Canada*. Read any Leaf history accounts or Canadian history books and you will find all these volumes with references to the iconic show that first began on radio and then made a seamless transition to television.

Beginning in the 1930s, the Leafs' Saturday night encounter at home has been a staple of Canadian entertainment. People would gather around their radios to listen to Foster Hewitt's accounts and descriptions of games played at Maple Leaf Gardens. There was not much in terms of entertainment options in those days and Hewitt seemed to make every game the Leafs played an epic encounter no matter who was playing or what the score happened to be. It was great timing for the Maple Leafs who were a very good team throughout the decade of the 1930s even though they only took the Stanley Cup on one occasion. The 1940s saw the team win the championship five times and helped ease the anguish of Canada being involved in World War II. Hewitt's *HNIC* games were often recorded, edited and then transmitted to the BBC in England to be broadcast to Canadian forces fighting overseas to bring the troops some good news about what was going on back home in Canada and provide an immense morale booster.

Legendary broadcaster Foster Hewitt. (Harold Barkley Archives)

By 1952 the grand invention called television came into being and *Hockey Night in Canada* became a country-wide favourite with eventual coast-to-coast coverage. Now people could see what Hewitt was describing and even though the whole game was not shown, fans were thrilled to see even just some of the action. The Leafs were not very good in the 1950s (just one Cup in 1951), but by the time 1960 rolled around the team was back in contention. Once again the Leafs' timing could not have been better as most Canadians had purchased a TV sometime in the early part of the decade—just in time to see the team win four Stanley Cups. Leaf players became heroes to an entire Nation and their performances on Saturday night were "must see" TV. It was here that the "Leaf Nation" was born as the boomer generation saw the Toronto club as winners year after year.

If the last two seasons (1963–64 and 1966–67) that saw the Leafs win the Stanley Cup is any indication, it is easy to see why the team became so popular. In '63–'64 they posted a 19–2–4 record (all home games) in the regular season on Saturday night and then go 4–1 (featuring two home contests including the seventh game of the finals) in the playoffs on the same evening of the week. The winning percentage for the 30-game total was 77 percent and they gained at least one-point 90 percent of the time. In 1966–67 the Leafs were 15–4–4 in the regular season and a perfect 3–0 in the postseason for games played on Saturday. Over those two seasons (including playoffs), the Leafs played a total of 56 games on *Hockey Night in Canada* and won 41 times (for a 73-winning percentage) while gaining at least one-point 85 percent of the time. The funny thing is the team struggled both those seasons but they were great on Saturday nights and good enough to win the Stanley Cup both years.

The tradition of gathering around to watch the Leafs on *HNIC* was passed on to another generation and then again to other generations as time passed. In the 2013 playoffs the Leafs drew 5.1 million fans (a new record since audiences were measured more accurately) to their TV screen on a Monday night for the seventh game of a playoff series versus Boston. "We're thrilled at how Canadians have overwhelmingly embraced CBC's coverage and joined the yearly tradition that is the Stanley Cup playoffs on *Hockey Night in Canada*," said Julie Bristow, an executive director at the CBC. It proved once again that *HNIC* is the Leafs show and that is unlikely to change since their biggest part of the Canadian population still lives in southern Ontario. How many more people might have watched had the Leafs beaten the Bruins and advanced further?

A new television deal signed late in '13 takes control of *HNIC* from the CBC and places it with Rogers. Rogers Communications would be wise not to mess with a good thing. Generations of Toronto fans loyal to their team is proof positive that *HNIC* has a special place in the hearts of all Maple Leaf fans—and to think it all started in the 1930s!

3 Conn Smythe to Bell and Rogers

When Conn Smythe put together a group to take over ownership of Toronto's hockey franchise in 1927, the team known as the St. Patrick's was not exactly doing well. It took a few short years with a name change to "Maple Leafs," plus building a hockey palace known as Maple Leaf Gardens to turn the fortunes of the franchise around. Smythe had proven he could put together a good hockey team when he successfully ran the New York Rangers for a short period prior to returning to Toronto. With the Maple Leafs he was ably assisted by Frank Selke, Squib Walker, Dick Irvin, and

Hap Day. Soon the Leafs were loaded with great talent and won the Stanley Cup in their first season at the Gardens—the 1931–32 campaign.

Smythe was a crusty curmudgeon who was to say the least tight-fisted financially and he never hesitated to remind his players how lucky they were to be paid to play hockey. He was also a very shrewd businessman who realized that at times he had to spend money to make more (the purchase of star defenseman King Clancy is a good example). Smythe was in charge of the Maple Leafs between '27 and '57 and in that time, they won the Stanley Cup seven times and should have won more in the 1930s when they dominated the NHL many times during the regular season. He would never let his team get embarrassed, and when it was time to make changes to the roster, Smythe always wanted what was best for his team to keep winning. He was also the one who gave assistant general manager Punch Imlach his blessing to go ahead and fire Toronto coach Billy Reay in November of 1958. That move started a new era of winning for the Maple Leafs under Imlach's guidance.

Smythe was formally bought out in 1961 by a group of three led by his son Stafford. John Bassett and Harold Ballard were the other partners and they reaped the success of the Leafs' great recruiting to win four more Stanley Cups by 1967. On the night the Leafs clinched the '67 championship Conn proudly boasted that the Smythe name was on the Cup a total of 11 times and no other family had such a distinction. The Leafs had been in the Stanley Cup final a total of 19 times between '27 and '67 and it looked like the good times could keep rolling. However, as the new trio became more prominent, problems developed and soon it was down to Ballard (a man Conn Smythe never liked) running the show. Stafford passed away at age 50 while Bassett refused to stay on board after his partners had been charged with tax evasion and the Board of Directors at Maple Leaf Gardens would not let him

Toronto owner Conn Smythe shakes the hand of Maple Leaf defenseman Bill Barilko. (City of Toronto Archives)

take over as President. Ballard's reign of error began in 1971 and lasted until his passing in 1990. Ballard turned the once beloved team into his own circus and even though he wanted to win, he had no clue how to do so. He always refused to hire the best managers and coaches available and the one time he did (going after Scotty Bowman in 1979), the attempt was rebuffed because of his reputation as a buffoon owner. He could treat some people very well and others very poorly but there was no doubt Ballard wanted to be the owner of the Maple Leafs first and foremost. The wins and losses did not seem to bother him enough but what mattered most to him was having his name in the newspaper or on television. Ballard was not leaving as long as he was alive.

Steve Stavro took over the Leafs after much wrangling over Ballard's will and things did improve a great deal under his ownership. The Leafs came as close to the Cup as they ever had since 1967 during Stavro's time but ultimately came up a little short. Soon Stavro had money difficulties and brought in other partners to help but eventually he made an exit when the cost of running the Maple Leafs became too high. By all accounts, Stavro did not skimp financially but when he ordered payroll reductions it was promptly done and he also declined to sign Wayne Gretzky—a move so baffling it defies logic—but was justified by saying Gretzky would not sell any more tickets in Toronto! It was also an easy way to say Gretzky's contract with the Maple Leafs would not fit under the payroll cuts necessary.

The Teacher's Pension Fund (of Ontario) took over as main owners and they were most concerned about return on their investment (as a pension fund should for their members) and not enough on winning. Minority owner Larry Tanenbaum admitted this in a newspaper interview when he said winning still mattered to the Teacher's Pension but generating revenue mattered more. The Teacher's leadership would pop out of the background every now and then to deny this was the case when they owned the team but the fact is their ownership of the Leafs was just too public for them to deal with in a proper way with conflicting agendas.

The Teacher's eventually got tired of running the team and taking all the heat so they sold their interest (at a huge profit—which was their plan all along) to Bell Canada and Rogers Communications—two companies that are normally fierce business rivals. It has not exactly been smooth sailing since the change, but upper management made a bold move by changing leadership, with Brendan Shanahan now in charge as President in a bid to bring back the glory days. It is unlikely the two companies will retain equal ownership of the Leafs for too long but at least Leaf fans can say top business people are in charge of the team and they know winning is the best way to keep the organization strong and stable going into the future.

4 The 1963–64 and the 1966–67 Marlies

When the Maple Leafs won the Stanley Cup in 1964 and 1967, it looked like their dynasty would go on for years but that was not the case. The 1963–64 junior Marlboros iced one of the best teams in history posting a 40–9–7 record during the regular season (notching 87 points in the process) before romping to the Memorial Cup championship. The team was filled with future Maple Leafs including the top three best point producers on the team which included Peter Stemkowski, Mike Walton and Ron Ellis. All three would go on to help the Leafs win the Cup in '67.

However, there were other players on the team who were expected to be good NHL players. Some of those included wingers like Wayne Carleton, Brit Selby, plus defensemen Jim McKenny and Rod Seiling. Goaltender Gary Smith was also expected to be a Maple Leaf in the future with Johnny Bower getting older and soon to retire. These five players added to the other three surefire future Leafs would have given the team a total of eight new recruits to mix in with whatever veterans were held over on the big club. It seemed like everything was in place with a succession plan but it did not quite work out that way.

First, Seiling was lost to the New York Rangers in the trade that landed Andy Bathgate and Don McKenney in February of 1964. Another promising defenseman in Arnie Brown was also gone in that deal leaving the Leafs two defensemen short. Brit Selby was the NHL's rookie of the year in 1965–66 and he looked promising after his first year. An injury derailed Selby (who had 52 points in 48 games for the Marlboros in '63–'64) and he never recovered in Toronto and became a somewhat marginal player for the rest of his career after he left the Maple Leafs before returning for another tour of duty. The same thing essentially happened to Carleton (a 42-goal scorer for the Marlies who was anointed as the best junior prospect in Canada by Stafford Smythe) when he suffered a knee injury and was soon dealt to Boston for Jim Harrison, a player of some promise because of his aggressiveness but too slow to make any major impact beyond being a third line centre.

McKenny was compared to Bobby Orr as a junior, but he was never able to get the same reviews for his work in the NHL. He was a good Leaf defender for many years as an offensive type of blue-liner but never the superstar the Leafs might have hoped for when he was a Marlie. As for Smith, he played a grand total of five games as a Maple Leaf before leaving for the Oakland Seals. In addition, the Leafs did not get much more out of left winger Brian Conacher (who had graduated from the Marlies in 1962) after his superb performance in the '67 playoffs. He was thought to be a solid third line winger with the ability to score and kill penalties, but he was soon gone as well.

Jim McKenny (left) was a great player for the Toronto Marlboros in 1963–64.
(Harold Barkley Archives)

As for the '67 Marlies (who posted a 23–15–10 record) they were not nearly as good as the '64 club but they had some promising players as well including Gerry Meehan, Doug Acomb, Mike Pelyk and Brian Glennie who led them to the Memorial Cup championship. Meehan however was soon dealt away to Philadelphia while Acomb one of the slickest junior talents (recording 93 points in 54 games for the 1968–69 Marlies), would play a grand total of two games for the Maple Leafs. Glennie and Pelyk were solid performers for the Leafs over many seasons but neither had the star status in the NHL that they enjoyed in junior hockey. But the biggest loss from the '67 junior champions was that star defenseman Brad Park was not signed by the Leafs, leaving him open to be taken by the New York Rangers in the 1966 amateur draft. Park would go on to have a great Hall of Fame career and was a perennial candidate for the Norris Trophy. No one is sure why the Leafs lost out on Park but it would seem the paperwork was never properly registered and it slipped through the cracks.

Put all these player losses and on-ice disappointments together and you have the beginning of the end of the Maple Leafs dynasty.

Punch Imlach and the June '67 Expansion Draft

The Stanley Cup–winning Leafs were on top of the world going into the expansion draft, after upsetting both the powerful regular season champion Chicago Black Hawks and archrival, the Montreal Canadiens, to win the franchise's 13ᵗʰ title. Whether it was over-confidence by the cocky general manager Punch Imlach or lack of preparation, the Toronto brass made curious, if not damaging personnel decisions leading up to the draft and on the big day itself.

Up front, Imlach retained Dave Keon, Frank Mahovlich, Ron Ellis, Bob Pulford, Jim Pappin, and Pete Stemkowski as sure things along with Brian Conacher and Mike Walton—both important players in the '67 championship. Walton would score 30 goals for the Leafs in 1967–68 so it was a good move to keep the skilled centre on board. This gave the Leafs more than two solid lines up front with age not really being a problem. Imlach convinced captain George Armstrong to announce his "retirement" prior to the draft in the hopes he would be left alone by the new teams.

Stalwart veterans like Red Kelly, Allan Stanley and Terry Sawchuk were left exposed in the expansion draft as was utility forward Larry Jeffrey and veteran defenseman Kent Douglas. Imlach should also have left veteran defenseman Marcel Pronovost available and protected Bob Baun but he was loyal to those who helped him win the '67 Stanley Cup. The other defenseman protected were Tim Horton and Larry Hillman, who was outstanding in the playoffs. Imlach felt he could not afford to keep veteran winger Eddie Shack at this point and dealt one of the most popular Leafs of all time to Boston for the effective but smallish winger Murray Oliver and $100,000 in cash—an extraordinary amount of money at the time. Imlach would have been better off to trade Shack for a netminder because the Leafs had little beyond Johnny Bower and Bruce Gamble ready to play in net.

While Montreal general manager Sam Pollock made side deals to keep the roster he wanted (the Habs would win the Stanley Cup in 1968 and 1969), Imlach made no such attempt to make similar arrangements with the GMs of the expansion teams, which might have allowed the Leafs to keep a player like Baun. Why Imlach was so inactive has never been explored fully and may lie in the rubble that the Leaf farm system became after '67 after a sellout of assets for cash. Their perennial championship teams in Rochester were stocked with players no longer under Leaf control. Not only was Imlach's ability to make pre-arranged trades hampered, but once Leaf-owned players were drafted by expansion teams, he curiously filled their spots in the ongoing draft with Rochester players that for the most part would never play in the NHL. In the process, Imlach lost several young players that would have been so helpful entering the 1970s when the NHL grew and the World Hockey Association became a threat.

In July of 1966, Robert Clarke, Merle Sweet and Larry Quinn, formed a civic group in Rochester to purchase the Rochester Americans for an estimated $500,000 from the Leafs. Included in the price was the ownership of 19 player contracts. In this complicated deal, a Rochester spokesman said that all the players that

Punch Imlach (second from left) was the coach and general manager of the Maple Leafs from 1958 to 1969. (York University Archives/Toronto Telegram Collection)

participated in the '66 Calder Cup playoffs were now Rochester property, with the exception of Jim Pappin and Mike Walton. Rochester GM/coach Joe Crozier, a longtime friend of Imlach's, would remain in his position as well as being offered stock in the team.

The Leafs would still have a working agreement with Rochester for three years and the contract allowed the parent Leafs to purchase two players a season from Rochester unless there was an immediate need for an emergency replacement player. All appeared straightforward, except for a stipulation that if any of the Rochester-owned players were selected in the expansion draft, Toronto would have to pay the Rochester owners $30,000 for each player lost. In turn, Rochester would pay a sum of $20,000 for a replacement player from the Leaf farm system. It was curious then how former Toronto-owned players officially sold to another organization could still be eligible for a future expansion draft—a deal with the potential for harmful ramifications.

Among the players listed as sold to Rochester were a number of veteran minor leaguers such as Dick Gamble, Stan Smrke, Les Duff, Norm Armstrong, Darryl Sly, Al Arbour and Don Cherry—none (with the exception of Arbour) with any real hope of playing in the NHL, expanded or not. However, there were a few prospects, including Stemkowski and Conacher, both of whom would play pivotal roles in the Leafs' Cup win the following year. Presumably, these players were purchased back from the Rochester team as part of the 1966 agreement.

Stafford Smythe and the Leaf owners, delighted at receiving $2 million from the expansion teams, would have been reluctant to give chunks of it back in compensation to Rochester. After all, the selling of the Rochester assets, followed a year later by cashing in the Victoria Maple Leafs in the Western Hockey League, was not in the name of player development. It was purely a desire to make money, a mistake that would contribute to the coming drop in team fortunes.

Imlach was thus hampered by the Leafs' obligations to Rochester, which affected his decisions about who to fill with on his list when he lost the exposed players. Two clues further support this. The newspapers of the day fail to mention the Rochester factor in their post-expansion reports, except for an Imlach quote at the end of one *Toronto Star* article. "We had to take certain players for Rochester," Imlach said, adding that, "Stanley, Armstrong and Kelly were the best men available when I protected them." *The Globe and Mail* also had a photo of the Leaf draft table with Imlach, Smythe, and Harold Ballard along with Robert Clarke "in animated discussion" according to the caption.

As a result, the Leafs lost out on young players such as Eddie Joyal, Mike Corrigan, Bill Flett, Lowell MacDonald, Mike Laughton, Darryl Edestrand and Larry Keenan. None of these players were stars but they played valuable roles for their respective clubs in the early years of the expansion era. The Leafs could have used this depth to add to their roster and to make more trades at the NHL level instead of worrying about re-stocking the Rochester Americans—a team they completely severed ties with a short time later. Toronto's netminding was in disarray and the defense was not much better with promising youngsters never achieving star status. The Leaf dynasty was in complete decline by this point and has never been quite the same despite numerous efforts to rebuild.

6 The Ultimate Road Trip

Mike Wilson, known as "The Ultimate Leafs Fan," embarked on a fantastic journey during the 2018–19 season by attending every Toronto home and away game including the playoffs—89 games in total. Reflecting on his road trip to the 30 other NHL cities, Mike found that "Leaf Nation" had no boundaries! The passion exhibited by Leaf fans at these games was more than he could have imagined. The experience will be detailed in his upcoming book, *The Ultimate Road Trip*.

Here are some of his observations:

The Best Arena:
"Little Caesars in Detroit, with Rogers Place in Edmonton and T-Mobile in Las Vegas a close second."

Best City to Visit:
"Nashville hands down, and Leafs Nation was prominently represented, taking over Broadway Street."

Most Surprising Venue for Leaf Fans:
"Anaheim. The Orange County ex-pats try to attend all the Canadian teams' games but the overwhelming favorite are always the Leafs."

Best Non-Hockey Moment:
"In Columbus, December 28, 2019, while exiting Nationwide Arena after a Leafs win, the brisk wintery air was filled with a trumpeter playing 'Oh Canada' and the departing Leafs fans singing the National Anthem."

Longest-Distance Fans:
"Two ladies from Australia who picked up hockey locally and then started following the NHL, adopting the Leafs as their team. They made the trip from Down Under to attend three games in Toronto."

Craziest Fan:
"The 50-something chap from Thunder Bay who snuck out of his house with his Leafs sweater tucked under his coat, jumped in his buddy's car, then made the six-and-a-half-hour drive to see the Leafs play in Minnesota."

Coolest Moment:
"Watching the 3-on-3 tourney in Minnesota on the outdoor rink across from the Xcel Energy Center. Seeing the players later heading to the bus with skates slung over their shoulders stopping to buy hot dogs at the concession stand. It was a reminder of the early days playing as youngsters."

Most Moving:
"At Scotiabank Arena, meeting the surviving members of the Humboldt Broncos hockey team."

"Wow" Factor:
"Entering every rink and seeing Leafs Nation sometimes 15 rows deep surrounding the visitors end during the pregame warm-up."

* * *

Mike found that the common theme was that Leaf fans were everywhere. He would find 'Leaf Talk' at the rink, a bar, walking the streets or waiting at a gate at the airport. Of course, there were some harrowing moments with flights, weather or lost uber drivers but all in all the experience was tremendous. He was taken back on how many fans from across the country were travelling to see the Leafs play around the league. Whether it's choosing a few games annually; targeting new rinks with the aim of attending a game in every venue or just making an annual excursion with a group combined with attending other sporting events, the key component was to cheer their team on wherever they played.

7 Brian Burke

When Richard Peddie convinced the Board of Directors at MLSE to fire John Ferguson, Jr. he did the right thing and gave himself a chance to rectify his own mistake. Ferguson was a good scout who was in way over his head as a rookie general manager in a city like Toronto, and bosses like Peddie did little to help him (not letting Ferguson tear down the roster after missing the playoffs in 2006 for example). Peddie named Cliff Fletcher as interim general manager which gave him more time to find viable candidates, although it became evident that the short-term boss was not going to be as stellar as he had been when he first took over the Leafs in 1991.

In his recent book Peddie said one of the people he spoke to was Scotty Bowman, arguably the greatest coach in NHL history. Bowman was considered for a much higher management position than coach with the Maple Leafs. He was going to oversee the entire operation and likely hire his own general manager and coach. Peddie said he did some checking around at places where Bowman had worked before and did not like the feedback he heard and therefore passed on hiring a hockey legend. He might have heard something along the lines of Bowman being very impulsive and wanting to make wholesale changes after a bad loss—at least that was the knock on Bowman when he worked for the Montreal Canadiens. However, Peddie did not elaborate so it is pure speculation just as Bowman's age might have been a factor.

Peddie says there was another unnamed candidate considered by the team and it might have been Beeton, Ontario, native Jim Rutherford who was the general manager of the Carolina Hurricanes. Toronto hockey fans will recall watching Rutherford play junior hockey for the Hamilton Red Wings and then saw the netminder play briefly (a total of 18 games) for the Maple Leafs in 1980–81. Hurricanes owner Peter Karmanos said he would not stand in Rutherford's way if he wanted to come to Toronto but it is likely the conservative Rutherford decided to stay where he was for family reasons although it must be stressed that this is pure speculation. Rutherford's experience and success (one Stanley Cup victory in 2006 plus another trip to the final in 2002) level would have been too hard to ignore.

However, another Stanley Cup winner (with Anaheim in 2007) made it known he was very interested in running the Maple Leafs and his name was Brian Burke. As the search (led by Toronto sports lawyer Gord Kirke) for the most viable candidate stalled, Peddie did not seem to have anyone with such a high profile to consider. It became a waiting game for Burke to be given the OK to leave the Ducks. Burke had all the attributes the Leafs were looking for and waited as long as they had to secure Burke's services with a multi-million-dollar deal over six years. Burke managed the Hartford Whalers, the Vancouver Canucks and the Anaheim Ducks and enjoyed various levels of success with each team. He had also worked at the NHL head office and one of his roles there was to act as the league disciplinarian. Plus, the man had a boastful personality with lots of colour to keep the Toronto media enraptured with his every word. It seemed like a perfect fit for all as he took the job in November of 2008.

Burke did not come to Toronto to let the grass grow under his feet and in his boldest move, he paid a heavy price for winger Phil Kessel. The trade sparked a great deal of controversy and Burke was always being prodded about it. He also kept Ron Wilson (his good friend and a man Burke once represented as an agent) behind the Leafs bench—a situation that became untenable as time passed. More trades were completed and free agents signed but the Maple Leafs did not make the playoffs as long as Burke was in charge. Soon all of his press conferences were cringe-worthy events as nobody could tell what Burke was going to spew next.

When new owners took over, they found Burke's style unbearable and dismissed him in January of 2013 just as the lockout-shortened season was about to begin. Many defended Burke but just as many were glad to see him go. The much more understated Dave Nonis took over and the Maple Leafs made the playoffs for the first time in eight years. Hiring Burke was something the Leafs had to try—it just did not work out the way it was supposed to.

Worst Leaf Trades

October 16, 1989—1991 first-round pick to New Jersey for Tom Kurvers

Kurvers had good offensive skills and accumulated 52 points for the Leafs in the 1989–90 season. But after tallying a mere three assists in 19 games the following season, he was traded to Vancouver. What made the deal look worse for GM Floyd Smith was that 1991 was the much-anticipated Eric Lindros draft year. The Leafs finished 19th out of 21 teams at the end of the 1990–91 season and while Lindros was chosen No. 1, the Devils happily took future Hall of Famer Scott Niedermayer third.

March 3, 2003—Alyn McCauley, Brad Boyes, and a 2003 first-round pick to San Jose for veteran Owen Nolan

Pat Quinn made this move to strengthen his team for a longer Stanley Cup run, but in seven playoff games Nolan failed to score even one goal. The 2003–04 season was Nolan's last with the Leafs, as he was unable to play the next two seasons because of injury. Boyes went on to have 26-, 43-, and 33-goal seasons after the trade.

July 4, 2006—Tuuka Rask to Boston for Andrew Raycroft

GM John Ferguson Jr. had the best goalie prospect outside the NHL, but he trades their 2005 first-round pick, Tuuka Rask, to Boston for Andrew Raycroft. The unsigned Raycroft was coming off an 8-win 19 loss season and a 3.71 GAA. The previous season he played in Finland with a 6.36 GAA in the playoffs. Less than two years later, Raycroft was placed on waivers by the Leafs. Rask became a star, adding a Stanley Cup, Vezina Trophy, All-Star nods, and Olympic medal to his résumé.

June 22, 2007—A 2007 first-round pick, a 2007 second-round pick, and a 2009 fourth-round pick to San Jose for goaltender Vesa Toskala and forward Mark Bell

Odd move since John Ferguson Jr. traded Rask for Raycroft a year earlier. Toskala, the Sharks backup, played well for the Leafs early but his play declined and he was dealt to Anaheim. Mark Bell, after scoring four goals in 35 games, was waived through the league. Trading draft choices is not a good strategy.

November 24, 2008—Alexander Steen and Carlo Colaiacovo to St. Louis for Lee Stempniak

Interim GM Cliff Fletcher makes a bad trade just prior to Brian Burke taking over. Steen, a former Leaf first-round pick, was a two-way player and deemed captain material. Adding another former first pick in defenseman Colaiacovo was just too much to give up. Stempniak was coming off a 13-goal season but had scored 27 goals the year before. Was he a 27-goal or a 13-goal scorer? Sadly, he was the latter and was soon traded to Phoenix. Steen has had 12 productive seasons with the Blues, winning a Stanley Cup.

More Questionable Deals:
May 23, 1968—Jim Pappin to Chicago for Pierre Pilote

Pilote played one year with Leafs then retired. Pappin scored 216 goals for the Hawks over the next seven seasons.

August 21, 1985—John Anderson to Quebec Nordiques for Brad Maxwell

Anderson was coming off 31-, 31-, 37-, and 32-goal seasons with the Leafs. Then had 29- and 31-goal seasons after he left. Maxwell played one year and then was traded for a fifth round pick.

October 1, 1999—Forward Fred Modin to Tampa Bay for defenseman Cory Cross
The big, 6'4" Modin had seasons of 32, 32, and 29 goals for the Lightning. Cross played three seasons as a third-pair defenseman before leaving for the Rangers.

Best Leaf Fighters

Pre-1970:
Orland Kurtenbach (Cudworth, Saskatchewan) Best stand-up boxer in league; destroyed Terry Harper and others.

Fern Flaman (Dysart, Saskatchewan) Heavyweight champion of the 1950s; beat them all: Fontinato, Howe, all the toughies.

Harry Watson (Saskatoon, Saskatchewan) Not many wanted to mess with him after he broke Murray Henderson's nose with one punch.

Bill Juzda (Winnipeg, Manitoba) Took on all comers: Maurice Richard, Ted Lindsay—and beat Gordie Howe.

Reg Horner (Lyndon, Ontario) NHL's "Bad Man," leading the league in penalties for seven straight seasons. When angry, watch out; kayoed Eddie Shore.

Honourable Mention:
Bob Baun (Lanigan, Saskatchewan)

Post-1970:
Wendel Clark (Kelvington, Saskatchewan) Based on size and courage: the toughest. Took on all the heavyweights and hurt people.

Tie Domi (Windsor, Ontario) Not the biggest fighter but could take a punch and return with haymakers that disabled many an opponent.

Tiger Williams (Weyburn, Saskatchewan) More of a grab and puncher, protected Sittler and McDonald, and a fighter that opponents didn't like to get in close with.

John Kordic (Edmonton, Alberta) Erratic personality scared opponents, and his left-handed punches hurt them.

Wade Belak (Saskatoon, Saskatchewan) Very effective enforcer and could play forward and defense.

(Note: Of the 10 listed top fighters, eight are from Western Canada and six from the province of Saskatchewan.)

Honourable Mention:
Colton Orr (Winnipeg, Manitoba)

10 Blue and White Disease

When the Maple Leafs hired Brian Burke, most Toronto fans were happy to have an experienced executive with a winning record (including one Stanley Cup title) sitting in the very high-profile general manager's chair. It did not work so well in reality and Burke could only muster a slightly below .500 record with no appearances in the postseason. Burke pointed out many problems and concerns he had during his tenure as the Leafs boss one of which he termed "blue and white disease."

Burke felt too many Leaf players were made into heroes whenever they had a good game or short periods of excellent performance. He thought the media was ready to erect statues to rather ordinary players who had experienced a short-term surge. The players would read or hear the accolades and soon believe they were better performers than they really were. There is some truth to Burke's assertion but the real blue and white disease is actually something entirely different. The real "illness" consists of Toronto general managers (including Burke) constantly overpaying in trades to the short- and certainly long-term detriment of the organization. This disease has been going on for a long time (since the 1960s) and only recently has there been a slowdown in the spread of this phenomenon which has plagued the Leafs for too long.

Blue and white disease actually begins in the offices of general managers across the NHL who exploit the pressure and scrutiny faced by those running the Maple Leafs. The best example to illustrate this point came in 1989 when the New Jersey Devils sent defenseman Tom Kurvers to Toronto for a number one draft choice. New Jersey general manager Lou Lamoriello (one of the shrewdest assessors of NHL talent) knew Kurvers was nowhere near worth a first-round pick, but he also realized the Leafs were in dire need of someone to run the power-play from the point. At most Kurvers was worth a third or maybe a second-round draft choice, but Leafs general manager Floyd Smith paid the higher price because he felt he had to do something to address the team needs. He was also reacting to the stated desire of Leaf coach Doug Carpenter who knew Kurvers from his days in New Jersey.

Not only did Smith give a number one pick, he gave it up for the following year 1991, when Eric Lindros was the prize of the Entry Draft. Smith honestly felt the Maple Leafs were not going to be so bad that they would be drafting so high again as they had for most of the 1980s, but Lou Lamoriello figured it would not be a bad thing to get an extra lottery ticket for the pick of the litter in '91. The trade did not look so bad in the 1989–90 season as Kurvers played reasonably well and the Leafs made it to the play-offs with a .500 record over the regular season. They were quickly disposed of by the St. Louis Blues in the opening round of the playoffs—a team they had dominated 7–1 in games won or lost over the regular campaign!

The next season was an absolute disaster for the Leafs forcing Smith to give away more youth for veteran players just to avoid the humiliation of turning over the top pick to the Devils. As it turned out, the Devils got defenseman Scott Niedermeyer with the third choice (a Hall of Fame inductee in 2013) who hoisted the Stanley Cup four times over the course of his illustrious career. Kurvers was soon gone and would be long forgotten if not for the New Jersey selection of Niedermeyer.

Lamoriello was not the only general manager to take advantage of the Leafs. Others include Serge Savard (who stole former first-round pick Russ Courtnall), Mike Milbury (who acquired first-round selection Kenny Jonsson and then got another first-round draft choice who turned out to be Roberto Luongo), Doug Wilson (taking two first-round draft choices in separate deals), Peter Chiarelli (who pilfered away former first-round pick goalie Tuuka Rask in one lopsided deal and then got an extra first-round draft choice in the deal for Phil Kessel) all for players mostly on the downside of their careers (like Owen Nolan) or those who proved to be poor NHL performers (like Vesa Toskala). All of the general managers smiled at the time of the deal and waxed about how they did not want to trade players like Mathieu Schneider, Mark Bell, Andrew Raycroft, and even John Kordic. However, the reality is they know the market pressures the Leafs are under and they took advantage to the highest degree possible. They are also keenly aware that they might not ever extract such a return if it was any other team.

11 Phil Kessel and Brian Burke

When Brian Burke took over the Maple Leafs in November of 2008, it was only a question of time before he would make a major move. Prior to the start of the 2009–10 season, Burke sent a total of three draft choices (two in the first round) to the Boston Bruins in exchange for 22-year-old right winger Phil Kessel who was a restricted free agent at the time. If the Leafs had simply signed Kessel to an offer sheet, they would have had to pay out three draft choices (only one first rounder, one second-round choice and a third-round pick) if the Bruins were not willing to match. There was no indication the Bruins wanted Kessel back and Boston coach Claude Julien was no fan of the slick winger. Instead Burke decided to secure Kessel's rights first (unwilling to wait to see what the Boston side would do with the offer sheet while claiming he did not do business that way) and thus ended up paying a heavier price. Burke sought no protection (he claims he did not even ask) if the Leafs should fall to the point where they would be picking very high (somewhere between first and fifth) in the 2010 Entry Draft. Burke's decision caused another year of angst for the entire organization as the Leafs plummeted in the standings and would ultimately miss out on a top prospect.

The best two players available in the '10 draft was Taylor Hall (chosen first overall by Edmonton) and Tyler Seguin, who would be taken by the Bruins with the Leafs top pick. If Burke had secured some protection (that is to say Toronto would have the option for one year of deciding to take the choice between first and fifth overall should they be in such a position), the Leafs would have been eligible to select the talented Seguin AND still have Kessel on the team. The Bruins would then get the next two first round picks from the Leafs without any strings attached to close the deal. Instead the Bruins were able to land Seguin (who was since traded to Dallas but not before winning a Stanley Cup in 2011) AND defenseman Dougie Hamilton, a highly regarded prospect with the other first-round choice.

Kessel was dogged by the media about how he would be forever linked to the players the Bruins chose in the deal to get his rights and Bruin fans would mockingly chant "Thank you Kessel" whenever the Leafs came to Beantown to get shellacked by the bigger and more aggressive Bruins. Giving a divisional opponent like

Brian Burke and Phil Kessel pose during a news conference on Saturday, September 19, 2009. (AP Images)

the Bruins such an advantage might not have happened if Burke had been more forceful and not so willing to give into Boston's demands to make the trade. Other teams started to put in protection clauses in trades after this deal was consummated because they could see the folly of what Burke had done.

However, it must be duly noted that Kessel performed more than admirably as a member of the Maple Leafs. He scored goals (156 in 364 games prior to the start of the 2014–15 season and finished in the top 10 in league scoring three times (including a career high 82 points in 2011–12 that saw him place sixth overall in NHL scoring). The Leafs were also much more competitive and almost edged Boston out in the first round of the 2013 playoffs.

Prior to the '13–'14 season (a season that saw him score 37 goals and total 80 points) Kessel signed a new eight-year contract at $8 million per season, showing a strong commitment to Toronto and the Maple Leafs. It was great to see a top player actually wanting to stay in Toronto and not watch him walk away like Tracy McGrady, Vince Carter (both left the Toronto Raptors basketball team), Roy Halladay, and John Farrell (both left the Toronto Blue Jays baseball club).

Kessel was later traded to Pittsburgh by the Leafs for a first-round pick and former first-rounder Kasperi Kapanen, with other picks and players mixed in.

The new Leaf general manager, the experienced Lou Lamoriello, traded the pick acquired for Kessel to Anaheim for the sorely needed number one goaltender, Fredrik Andersen. Together with the skilled Kapanen, the Leafs salvaged something good from the controversial Phil Kessell trade.

12 Best Maple Leaf Trades

1. October 10, 1930—King Clancy from Ottawa for Art Smith, Eric Pettinger, and $50,000 cash
   Clancy was colourful and talented and helped make the Leafs a perennial Stanley Cup contender.
2. February 28, 1943—Ted Kennedy from Montreal for Frank Eddolls
   Ted Kennedy won five Stanley Cups, was captain, and may be the best Leaf of all time.
3. November 2, 1947—Max Bentley and Cy Thomas from Chicago for Gus Bodnar, Gaye Stewart, Bud Poile, Ernie Dickens, and Bob Goldham
   Leafs get the best player in the trade in Max Bentley and win three more Stanley Cups.
4. February 10, 1960—Red Kelly from Detroit for Marc Reaume
   Four-time Stanley Cup winner in Detroit, wins four more with the Leafs. A real steal.
5. September 19, 1991—Grant Fuhr, Glenn Anderson, and Craig Berube from Edmonton for Vincent Damphousse, Luke Richardson, Peter Ing, and Scott Thornton
   Fuhr was later traded for another good return and Anderson supplied speed and goal scoring.
6. January 2, 1992—Doug Gilmour, Jamie Macoun, Ric Nattress, Rick Walmsley, and Kent Manderville from Calgary for Gary Leeman, Michel Petit, Jeff Reese, Craig Berube, and Alexander Godynyuk
   Leafs get best player in Gilmour, Macoun solidifies the defense, trade leads to Stanley Cup runs of 1993 and 1994.

7. **February 2, 1993—Dave Andreychuk, Darren Puppa, and a first-round pick from Buffalo for Grant Fuhr**
   Enables Leafs to use Felix Potvin as their number one goalie. Andreychuk scored over 50 goals twice.

8. **June 28, 1994—Mats Sundin, Todd Warriner, Garth Butcher and a first-round pick from Quebec for Wendel Clark, Sylvain Lefebvre, Landon Wilson, and their first-round pick**
   Essentially Sundin for Clark. Sundin becomes Leaf top scorer, captain, and HOF player.

9. **June 23, 2012—John Van Riemsdyk from Philadelphia for Luke Schenn**
   Flyers trade a No. 2 overall pick for a No. 5 overall pick. An absolute steal for the Leafs.

10. **June 19, 2015—Zack Hyman from Florida for Greg McKegg**
    Another hijacking. Hyman adds intangibles that the Leafs need.

Honourable mention acquisitions by the Maple Leafs from other deals: Eddie Shack (1960), Bernie Parent (1971), Rick Vaive & Bill Derlago (1979), Dion Phaneuf (2010).

13 Dion Phaneuf

On January 30, 2010, the Vancouver Canucks came into Toronto for a Saturday night encounter with the Maple Leafs. The home side came out strong and scored three times before the opening stanza was done. Sniper Phil Kessel scored twice while fourth liner Jamal Mayers added another to give the Maple Leafs a 3–0 lead. Toronto netminder Vesa Toskala who was having a difficult season looked good in the opening period while the Leafs' attack forced Canucks goalie Roberto Luongo out of the Vancouver net. He was replaced by former Leaf goalie Andrew Raycroft, a netminder the Leafs had basically discarded.

Vancouver scored the only goal of the second period to make it 3–1, but anyone watching the game could see the Canucks surging while the Maple Leafs were clearly sagging. In the third period Vancouver scored four times (one into an empty net) to win the game 5–3. The Vancouver line of Alex Burrows and the Sedin twins (Henrik and Daniel) basically took over the game and the Toronto side had no response. Not one Maple Leaf player stepped up to do anything while Toskala folded up once again. The loss put the Leafs in last place in the Eastern Conference with just 45 points and only 17 wins. It all seemed very hopeless for the Maple Leafs.

However, the very next day Toronto general manager Brian Burke made a couple of bold moves and changed the complexion of the Maple Leafs for the short and long term. First, he sent Matt Stajan, Ian White, Nicklas Hagman, and Mayers to Calgary for defenseman Dion Phaneuf, forward Fredrik Sjostrom, and prospect Keith Aulie, at the time a highly regarded defenseman. Burke then sent forward Jason Blake and goaltender Toskala to Anaheim for former Conn Smythe Trophy winner goalie J.S. Giguere. In less than 24 hours after the meltdown versus Vancouver, the Maple Leafs were a different team.

The key acquisition from the Toronto point of view was Phaneuf who was a Norris Trophy runner-up just two seasons previously. Young at 24 years of age, the Maple Leafs firmly believed the big (6'3", 214 pounds) blueliner would regain his form in Toronto. The Leafs especially liked that Phaneuf was a physical type of defenseman who would give them some backbone along the blueline because Toronto was simply too easy to play against. "This guy is a warrior," Burke said of Phaneuf. "He's got a cannon for a shot and he plays the game hard. He's a big open ice hitter

Dion Phaneuf (Getty Images)

and he's a quality person." The Leafs had given up some offence to make the deal but nobody of any great significance. Defenseman of Phaneuf's caliber do not come available very often and the Leafs had to move quickly to close the deal.

Phaneuf's time in Toronto had been a bit of a rollercoaster ride but there is no doubt number 3 had given the team some character along the blueline. For some fans Phaneuf did not do enough, but he ate up a lot of minutes (usually over 25 minutes per game) and he was most often pitted against the best players on the other team. Phaneuf had also assumed the captaincy of the team and his teammates seemed comfortable with the "C" being pinned to Phaneuf's jersey. Phaneuf was always willing to stand up and deal with the media and did not shrink from the high scrutiny he had to deal with in Toronto. In 2013 the Maple Leafs made it back to the playoffs and Phaneuf's performance (28 points in 48 games) was a big reason why Toronto was finally back in the postseason. Phaneuf rarely missed a game and in the 2013–14 campaign, he had a plus/minus rating of plus-18 after 56 games played! However, a terrible late season collapse by Phaneuf and the entire team (only two wins over the final 14 games of the season) saw his rating drop to a mere plus-3.

Burke is now long gone from the Toronto hockey scene but he did give Maple Leaf fans a team leader for the years Phaneuf was in Toronto. And to think it all started after an ugly loss to the Vancouver Canucks!

14 Five Oddities at Leaf Games

1. **"Brown Ice" (November 30, 1963, vs Detroit Red Wings)**
When *HNIC* signed on at 8:30 PM, viewers were surprised to see that the ice surface was dark and choppy in appearance. When a rodeo takes over the floor the day before, with elephants leaving their deposits, it would be a challenge to get the ice surface ready for the game the next day. And there is always the worry of injuries on bad ice. Unfortunately, Detroit's goalie, Roger Crozier, playing in his first NHL game, suffered a broken jaw when a Frank Mahovlich slapshot hit pavement in a thin patch of ice and deflected up at his face. The game should never have been played under those conditions.

2. **"Firecracker or Bomb" (February 3, 1962, vs New York Rangers)**
It was a good thing that this incident occurred in 1962 and not in 2020, as the game would have been cancelled immediately. In the darkness in the rink while the national anthem was played, an explosive object was thrown from the stands to the ice, landing close to the Leaf bench. Linesman Matt Pavelich and Leaf defenseman Bob Baun suffered slight burns. Was it a prank gone wrong? The perpetrator was never caught.

3. **"The Unknown Coach" (March 3, 1979, vs Philadelphia Flyers)**
Unpredictable Leafs' owner Harold Ballard unintentionally revealed that he was a fan of "the Unknown Comic" from *The Gong Show*, an act which became a hit in 1979. Where else would he get the idea of having newly rehired coach Roger

Neilson wear a bag over his head prior to the game? Harold did some odd things but this has to be one of the strangest. Fortunately, Neilson didn't follow through with the gag.

4. **"The Streaker" (March 12, 1980, vs St. Louis Blues)**
"Streaking" at a sporting event had been a fad in the 1970s. So, it was a surprise when a Leaf fan jumped over the glass wearing only socks and carrying a "Maple Leafs #1" sign. He cavorted around centre ice for around 15 seconds before he was escorted off the ice by the police constables. It was a first at this rink and he drew a rousing ovation from the crowd, including Harold Ballard and the visiting St. Louis Blues.

5. **"Waffles" (December 9, 2010, vs Philadelphia Flyers)**
Toronto's "Finest" were quick to lay a "mischief" charge on a Leaf fan who was upset with the poor play of his team in a 4–1 loss to the Flyers. Charges were later dropped. But what was the crime? The frustrated fellow only threw waffles on to the ice to show his displeasure. Leaf defenseman Francois Beauchemin escaped injury when the soft and soggy "Eggo" was hurled at him from the Platinum seats at the Air Canada Centre. The significance of throwing waffles? Its anybody's guess.

15 Richard Peddie, Tim Leiweke, and Dave Nonis

Richard Peddie was not expecting to be named President and Chief Executive Officer of Maple Leaf Sports and Entertainment organization in October of 1998. Peddie held similar titles for the Toronto Raptors of the National Basketball Association starting in

1996 but when the Maple Leaf Gardens Limited (owners of the Maple Leafs) took over the basketball team and the arena project that was going to house the Raptors, he truly believed he was going to be dismissed. Much to his surprise he was offered the new roles at MLSE and he was a constant fixture with the organization for the next 15 years until he left on December 31, 2011.

Peddie was not really a sports executive although he did have experience running Toronto's domed stadium (then known as Sky Dome) plus some knowledge of sports television when he headed a communications company. Peddie was also involved in securing an NBA franchise working alongside Larry Tanenbaum who sought to bring basketball to Toronto. Otherwise his main experience was in marketing and sales and he was especially strong when he worked for the company that made Hostess potato chips. Peddie oversaw the entire operation that became responsible for the Maple Leafs, Raptors, Marlies (AHL hockey) and Toronto FC (soccer) plus the management of the Air Canada Centre which replaced Maple Leaf Gardens as the main sports (and entertainment) centre in the city of Toronto.

During his time at the helm of MLSE the organization grew in leaps and bounds and in a variety of areas. Three television channels were created (including Leafs TV), real estate became another venture for the company via the sale of condominiums and the development of Maple Leafs Square just outside the ACC. One of the largest sports bars was opened right next to the Maple Leaf Square while another arena (Ricoh Coliseum) saw the Leafs have a significant say in the management of its operation. The Leafs also created a superb practice and training facility when they opened the MasterCard Centre in lower Etobicoke. BMO Field became home to the soccer team and they developed a high-end training facility to produce future Canadian soccer players. It was quite an ambitious plan and it became clear the Maple Leafs were no longer the sole (or even main) focus of the organization. None of the new ventures ever had the words "money loser" attached to them but Peddie missed the most important thing—the teams had to win— and except for some early success from the hockey team, all the teams could be charitably described as big losers.

As the leader of the organization it was quite apparent that Peddie had no clue how to build a winner and chose poor leaders for each of his teams. He did let the executives he hired run their respective teams for the most part but one poor decision after another kept the losing foremost in the minds of Toronto fans. Peddie survived three ownership changes but none really complained about the job he was doing because the profits from all the new ventures were strong. In short MLSE became all about profits and business and not so concerned about winning (at least not to the point where they would do something significant—like going way over budget for example). Salary caps only gave the Peddie led organization a handy excuse to say "We are spending to the maximum allowed." But the Toronto sports fan did not want to hear those rationalizations and many sought to have Peddie dismissed. Eventually he said that he got tired of all the losing and finally announced his departure.

A search conducted by MLSE led to the hiring of American-born Tim Leiweke who had enjoyed great success in Los Angeles with both hockey and soccer. Brash and confident in style, Leiweke promised changes (especially to the basketball and soccer teams) and thought the Maple Leafs were going to be steady and strong under the leadership of general manager Dave Nonis, a quiet, thoughtful type not prone to going over the edge. Leiweke was bullish on Toronto and that was a refreshing change considering free agents had been shunning the city for some time. He promised to spend so that the teams had a great chance to win. Leiweke made one mistake by trying to tear down the past (by removing photos of Maple Leaf greats), but he quickly realized that was an error.

However, his point that all the teams under his control had to win now (in particular the Maple Leafs) was not lost on Toronto sports fans who clearly deserve to be rewarded. It seemed MLSE now had a person running it who cared about winning first and foremost and that was a refreshing change Leiweke could not possibly do worse than Peddie (who no doubt had a top business mind) when it came to winning. Leiweke's first major move with the Maple Leafs was to hire Hall of Fame player Brendan Shanahan as team president in April of 2014. Maybe some championships will be in seen in Toronto in the near future.

16 Best Late-Round Draft Picks

Pat Boutette (1972)—Ninth round, 139th overall. Popular winger didn't let his size hamper his aggressive style. Valuable member of Leaf teams in the late '70s.

Dimitri Mironov (1991)—Eighth round, 160th overall. Member of the Leaf playoff runs in the early '90s, teamed with Bob Rouse on defense. Good offensive skills.

Sergei Berezin (1994)—10th round, 256th overall. Maybe he didn't pass the puck much, but he scored a ton of goals for the Leafs in five seasons.

Danil Markov (1995)—Ninth round, 223rd overall. Yet another Russian. Danil played a North American style and was a regular defenseman with the Leafs in the late '90s.

Tomas Kaberle (1996)—Eighth round, 204th overall. One of the best late-round picks ever. Not expected to make the team, lasted 12 years as a top two defenseman.

Anton Stralman (2005)—Seventh round, 216th overall. Swedish reporters said he was the next Nicklas Lidstrom—not quite. But he did excel with other teams as a top 4 defender.

Carl Gunnarsson (2007)—Seventh round, 194th overall. Played five seasons of steady defense for the Leafs.

Connor Brown (2012)—Sixth round, 156th overall. Top scorer in junior proved he could play and score in the NHL. Good numbers for a player with no power-play time.

Andreas Johnsson (2013)—Seventh round, 202th overall. Scored a surprising 20 goals in his first regular season with the Leafs after leading Marlies to the Calder Cup

17 Nazem Kadri

A few days before the Maple Leafs were going to take on the Dallas Stars at home on December 5, 2013, Toronto centre Nazem Kadri learned that his grandfather who had the same name passed away at the age of 76. Kadri missed the Leafs game against the San Jose Sharks as a result of the passing but was ready two nights later when the Stars came in for a Thursday night contest at the Air Canada Centre. He was hopeful this was a game that could be a tribute to his grandfather's memory.

The Leafs were a team wrecked with injuries especially at the centre position (Tyler Bozak and Dave Bolland were both absent from the lineup due to injuries) so coach Randy Carlyle gave Kadri the number one centre spot between sharp shooting wingers Phil Kessel and James van Riemsdyk for this game. The contest remained scoreless into the second period when Kadri scored to give the Leafs a 1–0 lead. The Leaf pivot found himself all alone in front of the Dallas goal and made no mistake putting it past goalie Kari Lehtonen.

The Stars tied it early in the third period and it looked like the Leafs had lost the momentum they had enjoyed in the middle frame. However, the Leafs got a power-play opportunity and Kadri redirected a perfect pass from defenseman Cody Franson to give the Leafs a 2–1 lead. Even though Dallas tied it before the end of regulation time, the Leafs got a goal from Trevor Smith in overtime to clinch a badly needed 3–2 victory. The win put an end to a five-game losing skid.

"It's definitely something that he (his late grandfather) would have loved to see," Kadri said afterward about his two-goal

Nazem Kadri (Getty Images)

performance. "The last couple of years there hasn't been a game that he missed. He is going to be dearly missed by my family." The elder Kadri had come to Canada from Lebanon in 1968 to begin a new life and ended up settling in London, Ontario. One of his sons, Samir, ended up liking hockey and Samir's son Nazem began playing hockey around the time he was seven.

"He's the guy that really built the opportunity for us," Kadri said about his grandfather. "If he didn't come over to Canada, I would have been born overseas and life would be a lot different." The 23-year-old budding star of the Leafs paid tribute to his grand-parent by saying the elder Nazem was "the Don" of the family.

It has not been an easy road to the NHL for Kadri despite being a number one draft choice (seventh overall) by the Leafs in 2009. He has had to work hard in the minors and then had to wait to get a centre ice spot on the big team which is his natural posi-tion. Kadri was not exactly a favourite of former Leaf coach Ron Wilson, but found more opportunity under the mentorship of Randy Carlyle. The Leafs coach found time to comment on Kadri and how he dealt with the passing of a very important person in his life. "Nazem's had a tough couple of days. Emotionally I think he's pretty drained. I think it's good to see him rewarded…Usually you go back to work and get back into the swing of things in life, it helps you to move on."

A character-testing game like Kadri had against Dallas went a long way to making him the player the Leafs had envisioned when they drafted him out of the London Knights of the OHL.

18 James van Riemsdyk

One of the great things about the Toronto uniform is how the Maple Leaf logo has changed over the years since Conn Smythe renamed the team from the St. Patrick's back in 1927. There have been a number of versions of the logo adorning the team sweater and due to the Leafs participation in the 2014 NHL Winter Classic, one version experienced a revival of interest. It was a sweater that was first used from 1927 to 1934.

Based in a rich blue background, the '27–34 sweater featured a 48-point white Maple Leaf logo with thick stripes on the arms and white stripe bands coming off each shoulder. The bottom of the jersey also featured white bands. This sweater was first revitalized for the 1996–97 season when the team celebrated the 65th anniversary of Maple Leaf Gardens. The '96–'97 team was not very good (winning 30 games and missing the playoffs), so the old-time sweater did not get much attention.

It was a different story on January 1, 2014, when there was lots of time to build up to the game versus Detroit. Plenty of fans were wearing the vintage jersey and it seemed to catch on much better this time around and Reebok did a great job of making sure the sweater looked sharp and authentic to its history. One player who thrived in the jersey was James van Riemsdyk.

"JVR," as he is often called, was acquired by the Leafs in a trade with Philadelphia which saw former first-round choice Luke Schenn go to the Flyers. Drafted second overall by the Flyers in 2007, van Riemsdyk was not fulfilling his promise in Philadelphia and the Leafs felt the same about Schenn (who was selected in 2008). In the shortened 2012–13 season, van Riemsdyk started a little slowly but came on to score 18 goals and total 32 points in

48 games played. His good performance brought more expectations for van Riemsdyk in 2013–14 and his work around the opposition net had him scoring 30 goals. He had a soft set of hands that make him the envy of many teams and JVR was more than willing to take the punishment required to screen opposing goalies.

James van Riemsdyk (AP Images)

One of his most important goals came in the New Year's Day contest when he swatted at a puck in mid-air and tied the outdoor game 1–1. The Leafs went on to win the contest 3–2 in a shootout and gave the Leafs two important points in the standings. The team wore the vintage sweater once again on January 18, 2014, on home ice against the Montreal Canadiens. The Leafs lost a 3–1 lead and looked to be headed for overtime and perhaps another shootout. But van Riemsdyk converted a perfect pass from Tyler Bozak past Montreal goalie Carey Price for the game winner. After he scored the goal van Riemsdyk tugged on the Leaf logo as a way of showing Montreal's P.K. Subban that the Toronto side does not like to be taunted.

"He (Subban) was kind of taunting our bench a little bit (after a Montreal goal)," van Riemsdyk said after the game. "I'm usually not one to engage in stuff like that but I was a little bit fired up." It also marked his second important tally wearing the classic Leaf jersey. The old sweater certainly looked good as the Leafs celebrated a victory over their long-standing rivals from Montreal.

As good as the '27–'34 sweater looked this time around, the Leafs should consider going back to their 35-point Maple Leaf logo which was used from 1937 to 1967 which saw them win nine of their 11 Stanley Cups. The '67 playoff sweater (with the Maple Leaf just like the one on the flag of Canada) is now the team's "third" jersey and that is a good idea. The regular game sweater which was redesigned in 2010 is quite attractive and pays homage to the glory days with logos on each shoulder and the stripes on the arms and bottom of the jersey. However the 35-point Maple Leaf on the sweater still remains the team's best effort at a unique logo and style. It should become the Leafs permanent logo once again and hopefully van Riemsdyk, who scored 30 goals in 2013–14, can fill the opposing nets using that classic jersey!

19 Troy Bodie, Terry Clancy, Brent Imlach, and Mike Walton

When the Maple Leafs signed free agent right winger Troy Bodie, it seemed like the team was doing a favour to the son-in-law of newly installed MLSE president Tim Leiweke. Bodie was originally drafted by the Edmonton Oilers in 2003 (278th overall) but never played a game for them. He was signed as a free agent by Anaheim and played 57 games for the Ducks from 2008 to 2011. Bodie also played briefly for the Carolina Hurricanes but was essentially a minor league player for the most part—including a stint with the Leafs minor league team when he played in 16 games for the Toronto Marlies in 2009–10. Bodie had played in 107 NHL games and recorded 11 points (6G, 5A) prior to the Maple Leafs signing him as a free agent on July 10, 2013.

Bodie's game revolved around his imposing size (6'4", 220 pounds) and his willingness to mix it up. It would have seemed that the Leafs had plenty of size and toughness already prior to the start of the 2013–14 season which raised questions about why the robust winger was signed by the team. However, Bodie showed enough at training camp to earn more of a look and earned on assist on opening night in Montreal when the Leafs beat the Canadiens 4–3. With the Leafs,

Leafs coach Randy Carlyle indicated Bodie was a pleasant surprise and the tough forward was also admired for his strong determination. "I think Troy Bodie has probably been the biggest surprise," Carlyle said. "He's made a contribution on the forecheck, he's made a contribution on the defensive side of it. He's a big, strong guy and he separates himself from a lot of people with his strong work ethic."

Bodie's skating was not smooth but he worked very hard to get where he had to go and then tried to make something happen.

He was quite willing to drop the gloves as needed and that also pleased the Toronto coach. Bodie's goal against the Jets on January 25, 2014, proved he can strike at opportune moments. The Leafs were down 4–1 at the time but when he snapped home a wrist shot to close the gap, the team picked up some life and gained a very valuable point in the standing. Bodie has shown that he was not a Maple Leaf just because of his father-in-law!! Bodie scored three times and added seven assists in 47 games with the Maple Leafs.

Bodie is not the only player in team history to have family ties to someone in the organization. Brent Imlach played in a couple of games with the Maple Leafs because he was the son of coach Punch Imlach. Terry Clancy, son of the legendary defenseman King Clancy, was a low scoring left winger and played in 86 career games as a Maple Leaf. Slick centre Mike Walton was a very good Maple Leaf player (191 career points in 257 games played) between 1965 and 1971 and was on the Leafs 1967 Stanley Cup team. He was also married to the niece of owner Stafford Smythe at the time, and that might have kept Walton on the team a little longer than some in management (especially Imlach) might have wanted. Eventually he was dealt to Boston in 1971 where he won another championship.

20 Forbes Kennedy and Matt Frattin

April 2, 1969, and May 13, 2013, are two dates that will live forever in the minds of Maple Leaf fans—for all the wrong reasons. The 1969 contest between the Maple Leafs and Bruins was the first game of the quarter-final playoff series between the two teams. It turned out to be one of the ugliest games in NHL history with the

Leafs being on the wrong end of a 10–0 shellacking given out by a Bruins team anxious to tear the Leafs apart.

The Bruins took advantage of some early Leaf penalties and scored three times in the first period alone. Led by Phil Esposito's six-point night (4G, 2A), the Bruins added four tallies in the second before knocking in another three in the final frame. The Leafs tried to turn the game into a giant brawl with fights in every period but it was all to no avail—the Bruins were both tough and talented. Toronto defenseman Pat Quinn knocked out hometown superstar Bobby Orr with a flying elbow in the second period but that only served to enrage the Boston faithful who wanted to get at the Leaf blueliner while he sat in the penalty box.

If that was not enough, Leaf forward Forbes Kennedy went wild in the third period after he tried to get back at Boston net-minder Gerry Cheevers who had tapped Kennedy across the ankles with his goalie stick. In the ensuing melee, Kennedy punched linesman George Ashley to the ice. Ashley recovered and was able to get back into the fray while trying to stop all the fights. In total, Kennedy, a journeyman player over his entire 12-year career, set an NHL playoff record (which he now shares) with eight penalties in one playoff game (totaling 38 minutes). His total included two fighting majors, a 10-minute misconduct and a game misconduct in the third period alone. It turned out to be Kennedy's last game as a Leaf (he had been acquired in a late season deal with Philadelphia in March of '69) and in the NHL as he was suspended for the next three games. The Leafs were eliminated in four straight and were deservedly out of the postseason. Kennedy never played another NHL game but was in the American Hockey League during the 1969–70 season with the Buffalo Bisons.

Fast-forward 44 years later to 2013 and the Leafs were back in Boston for a seventh and deciding game in the first round of the playoffs. Toronto had fought back valiantly after being down 3–1 in games to even the series. It looked like the Leafs had the momentum and a chance to redeem the organization's pride against the Bruins who had defeated the Leafs in 1972 and 1974 in the somewhat same brusque fashion as in '69. The Leafs were up 4–1 in the third period before the Bruins scored to make it 4–2. The Leafs then made the mistake of trying to just hold on for the final 10 minutes of the game. It would prove to be a flawed strategy but if forward Matt Frattin had converted on a breakaway opportunity, all would have been well.

Selected 99th overall by Toronto in 2007, Frattin had worked his way up to the big team in a third line role after excelling with the Toronto Marlies in the 2012 playoffs (10 goals and 13 points in 13 games played). The 6', 180-pound right winger had displayed something of a scoring touch with 15 goals in 82 career games as a Maple Leaf. He had not scored in the '13 playoffs but a golden opportunity came up with the Leafs protecting their two-goal lead. Frattin came straight up the middle of the ice on Boston goalie Tuuka Rask and was in alone. A backhand attempt saw the puck roll off Frattin's stick with just 3:32 to play. His chance to put the game away failed and it gave the Bruins an opportunity to stage a miraculous finish.

The Bruins made the most of the reprieve and scored two late goals to tie the game (making it 4–4 at 19:09 of the period) before winning the game 5–4 in overtime over the reeling Leafs. A goal by Frattin would have surely ended any hopes of a Boston comeback but there was no good bounce for the Leafs in the closing moments of the seventh game. Before the start of the next season Frattin was traded to the Los Angeles Kings in a deal to secure goalie Jonathan Bernier.

Forbes Kennedy and Matt Frattin will always be remembered for two inglorious endings in Boston. Will the Leafs ever get revenge over the Bruins?

Alex Steen and Ron Wilson

When the Maple Leafs selected forward Alex Steen 24th overall in 2002 they had very high hopes for their top choice. He was seen as a prospect with great bloodlines since his father Thomas was one of the best ever Winnipeg Jet players (and a one-time co-captain of the Winnipeg club before they moved to Phoenix). Alex was born in Winnipeg but played most of his junior hockey in Sweden where his father came from originally. Never a great offensive producer, Steen was still valued for his all-round game and a skill set that one day might make him a very good or even a star player in the NHL.

Steen joined the Leafs for the 2005–06 season and did not disappoint by scoring 18 goals and 45 points in 75 games played as a 21-year-old rookie. The Leafs coach at the time was Pat Quinn and the legendary mentor saw a bright future for the youngster and even touted that the Leafs may have found a future captain. The next two seasons did not see a spike in Steen's offensive numbers and he also looked at little too tentative on the ice but he still scored a total of 30 goals and 77 points over a couple of seasons.

However, when the 2008–09 season began the Leafs were now coached by Ron Wilson, a former Leaf player and long-time NHL coach. To put it bluntly Wilson was never a coach shy of opinions and his view was that Alex Steen would never amount to much as a Maple Leaf and was seeing only spot duty while helping out with penalty killing chores. Wilson also had a particular disdain for another first-round draft choice (17th overall in 2001) in defenseman Carlo Colaiacovo, a player he believed was so injury prone because his body was not in NHL condition. The St. Louis Blues offered the Leafs winger Lee Stempniak a one-time 27-goal scorer in exchange for the two former number one draft picks. Toronto

Alex Steen celebrates a goal. (AP Images)

general manager Cliff Fletcher consulted Wilson on the deal since he knew more about Stempniak having seen him play more often in the Western Conference. Naturally, Wilson gave his blessing to the proposed swap and the two for one trade was completed November 24, 2008. Wilson would chortle that it only took the two players the Leafs gave up to land what they thought was a top six forward.

With the benefit of hindsight ten years later, it is easy to see that once again a hasty decision cost the Leafs a very good player. Colaiacovo never matched his potential even as he played for the Blues and later on the Detroit Red Wings (and he was back in St. Louis for the 2013–14 season). Stempniak was really a third line offensive player who could never match his one great season in St. Louis. The Leafs soon gave him away to Phoenix for two low draft choices (which were used in other deals) despite the fact he had 14 goals for the Leafs during the 2009–10 season.

Steen on the other hand has been a steady and solid performer for the Blues from the moment he arrived there. His offensive production has been a little up and down, but he has recorded seasons of 24 and 20 goals and in 2013–14 he had a career high in goals (33) and points (62) despite having concussion issues to deal with. He was named to Sweden's 2014 Olympic roster and helped the Blues win the Stanley Cup in 2019.

Steen was regarded so highly by the Leafs at one point that they refused to put him in a deal that would have landed them all-star defenseman Chris Pronger who was with Edmonton at the time. Now they lament the loss of a good player all because one coach could not find any potential in Steen. It is now clear how wrong Mr. Wilson was and how it spoke volumes of his failed time in Toronto as head coach highlighted by no playoff games in nearly four seasons behind the Leafs bench.

22 "Leafs Nation Network" and Mapleleafs.com

As the new century began, the technological revolution on how sports coverage was going to be delivered to the fans was in full flight. The Maple Leafs were ahead of the curve and applied for a specialty digital channel devoted specifically to its organization and especially to the Leaf hockey club. The application was approved by Canada's governing media regulator, the CRTC, and Leafs TV was launched on September 7, 2001 with John Shannon (formerly executive producer of Hockey Night in Canada) at the helm.

One of the biggest attractions to the digital station in the first year of Leafs TV operations was the very popular *Classic Games* show which would air a Maple Leafs game from the past twice a week. Fans could now see many of the glorious moments in Leaf history including nights when they won the Stanley Cup in 1963, 1964 and 1967. Other original programming included *Once a Leaf* which interviewed a former player while *Maple Leaf IQ* focused on a trivia about the team.

The station also started showing a few current Maple Leafs regular season games for those who subscribed and by the 2013–14 season, a total of 17 regular season games were only available to viewers of Leafs TV. It was thought that once Leafs TV was established that all but the Saturday night games would be shown on the specialty channel. But that has not happened and likely will not. The television deal struck between the NHL and Rogers Communications may have a large say in the future of Leafs TV, now called 'Leafs Nation Network' but it is likely to stay around in some form for many years to come.

Pregame and post-game shows of all Maple Leaf games dominate the station's programming while the ever-popular *Game in an*

Hour replays all Toronto games in just 60 minutes—one of the best ideas ever. *Leafs Today* focuses on the game being played that night with interviews featuring players and the head coach. As an added bonus select Toronto Marlies games are shown on the channel. If anything, significant is happening with the Maple Leafs, then Leafs Nation Network is one of the best sources of information around for all Toronto hockey fans.

MapleLeafs.com is another excellent source of information for fans of the team. Available worldwide on the Internet, the fan friendly site gives something for everybody with daily updates, features, commentary, game reviews, video highlights and provides links to other social media sites such as Facebook and Twitter. The site also features plenty of historical information and highlights and gives a link to follow the Toronto Marlies as well.

23 Maple Leaf Square and Real Sports Bar

Getting together with other fans is one of the best aspects of being a sports enthusiast. Maple Leaf fans like to get together and share the bond of cheering for the blue and white and while there are many locations to choose from, two recent additions seem to have stolen the spotlight.

Located just outside the, Scotiabank Arena, Maple Leaf Square is a 20,000 square foot atrium which has the main feature of a 50 by 80-foot video screen showing major sporting events and of course Toronto hockey games (home and away). The Leafs have had plenty of interactive activities at the Square (including alumni visits) but it is fast becoming one of the best places to be for those who do not have a ticket to the game or for those who want to be with other die-hard fans when the Leafs are in enemy buildings.

Maple Leaf Square did not have much of an impact until the 2013 playoffs when the Leafs lost a hard fought seven-game series to the Boston Bruins. The Leafs had been absent from the postseason for seven consecutive years and their first playoff appearance since 2004 brought out numerous Toronto fans from everywhere. Many of them gathered around the large screen and cheered for their team. When the Leafs scored a goal, the television cameras captured the reaction from the Square and it was quite loud and wild for every Leafs goal! Toronto police estimated there were thousands of fans in Maple Leaf Square and it has become something of a place to be, especially for those who find the cost of tickets to Leaf games too prohibitive. The real fun is watching a game outdoors with a group all wanting to see the Maple Leafs triumph. The status of Maple Leaf Square was only enhanced when the Toronto Raptors drew large crowds to the same location during the 2014 NBA playoffs and then the 2019 run to the championship.

Another welcoming place is the Real Sports Bar located beside Scotiabank Arena with Maple Leaf Square a few feet away. A 39-foot high definition screen is the main attraction to this sports bar but there are 199 other screens to please any sports fans taste. The food and drinks are typical of what you would find at any sports bar with the food portions made just the right size. The atmosphere is highly charged for most Maple Leaf games and the bar was rated the number one sports bar in North America just after it opened by ESPN—the most highly respected voice of sports in United States—quite a compliment! The service is very good to excellent and gives Maple Leaf fans another great place to gather together. One word of caution for game nights—reserve early!

24 Five Great Sports Bars to Watch a Game

1. **Real Sports Bar**—Conveniently located right next to Scotiabank Arena.
2. **The Bottomline Restaurant and Bar**—on Front St. near Scotiabank Arena—the place to be for hockey events with former players mixing in with the crowd.
3. **Wendel Clark's**—Former Leaf great's main location is in Vaughan and features many great Clark photos.
4. **Wayne Gretzky's**—Great downtown location with Gretzky memorabilia.
5. **Wegz Stadium Bar**—Northwest of the city. Features non-stop action on game nights.

25 Ted Kennedy

In September of 2001, the Maple Leafs announced a list of 25 players who were selected as the best of all time. Fourteen selectors made up from a variety of writers, broadcasters, managers, and other hockey experts were assigned the task of picking the best 25 players in Maple Leaf history. The selectors were not required to rank the players in any way rather they had to just simply pick 25 top Maple Leafs. Ultimately this group did a very good job and the greatest Maple Leafs were honoured by the organization one night before a home game. Syl Apps, George Armstrong, Turk Broda, Ted Kennedy, Dave Keon, Frank Mahovlich, Darryl Sittler, Mats

Sundin and Rick Vaive were but some of the players listed. The list was introduced alphabetically and the listing is shown in the same manner in the Maple Leafs media guide.

In 2007 veteran hockey writers Mike Leonetti and John Iaboni decided to do much the same exercise once again—only this time

Ted Kennedy with the 1951 Stanley Cup. (City of Toronto Archives)

each selector had to rank the players they chose in order of significance. The 14 selectors (it just worked out there were the same number) had to rank the players they selected from 1 to 100. The lower the number (much like a golf game) next to the player on the ballot, the higher he would rank on the all-time list. Some of the selectors were the same as the group who decided the 25 top Maple Leafs in '01 (such as the legendary *Toronto Star* writer Milt Dunnell who at 102 years of age at the time had seen every player on the ballot in action) plus a few new faces to make this committee a little different. However, when it was all analyzed in *Maple Leafs Top 100* (Raincoast Books of Vancouver), the top 25 remained the same names, only now they had a ranking.

The second group of selectors chose Dave Keon as the best Maple Leaf of all time with Ted Kennedy a close second. It is hard to argue with the selection of Keon who may have been the most complete hockey player of all time to wear the blue and white. Consideration has to be given to the fact that all the selectors would have seen Keon play on television while only three of the selectors would have seen Kennedy play on television and that would not have been during his prime years.

Kennedy should probably get more consideration as the best Maple Leaf of all time based on a host of factors. He is only one of two players (Broda is the other) in team history to play on five Stanley Cup winning teams, and he still holds the team record for most points in the Stanley Cup final (23 points in 26 games played). Kennedy was a Maple Leaf for his entire career (560 points in 696 games played) and is only one of two Maple Leaf players to win the Hart Trophy as the NHL's MVP. More than anything else, Kennedy was renowned for his leadership skills and he was named team captain in 1948. Perhaps the most dramatic words in Kennedy's favour come from Toronto manager Conn Smythe who called the gritty player the "quintessential" Maple Leaf.

It was a very interesting comment from Smythe considering he was very upset that the Leafs had sent defenseman Frank Eddolls to Montreal to get the rights to Kennedy who had never played for the Canadiens. Smythe was also someone who appreciated Keon's great talent (he made it known to Keon that he did not like the way owner Harold Ballard had treated the Toronto star), but he never wavered from his opinion about Kennedy.

26 Bill Barilko

When a sports franchise like Toronto's hockey team has won 13 championships, (11 Stanley Cups under the name Maple Leafs), over their illustrious history, it might be hard to pick out a single moment as the greatest in team history. Such is not the case with the Leafs whose signature moment came on April 21, 1951 when they defeated their greatest rival on home ice to win the Stanley Cup.

The Leafs and the Montreal Canadiens played a Stanley Cup final for the ages in 1951 when each game of the series went into overtime. Toronto won the opener on home ice at Maple Leaf Gardens with an overtime winner from the stick of Sid Smith. Montreal legend Maurice Richard tied the series with his overtime goal the next game but then the Leafs went into Montreal and won the next two games on extra time goals by Ted Kennedy and Harry Watson. Those wins gave the Leafs a chance to secure the Cup on home ice during a Saturday night contest at the Gardens.

Toronto had to get a late goal (with the goalie on the bench for an extra attacker) by Tod Sloan to tie the game 2–2 and send the fifth straight contest between the Habs and Leafs into another

Bill Barilko (next to the Montreal goalie) has just scored the greatest goal in Maple Leaf history. (City of Toronto Archives)

overtime session. The Leafs came out determined to end the game and capture their fourth Cup in five years. They swarmed into the Montreal end of the ice and Leaf forward Howie Meeker did some good work behind the Montreal net while fighting off big Tom Johnson of the Canadiens, one of their best defensemen. Watson took a swipe at the puck but the loose disk lay tantalizingly in the face-off circle when a Leaf defenseman decided to gallop in from the blueline and take a shot at ending the game.

Bill Barilko was a tough, rugged defenseman who had joined the Leafs during the 1946–47 season. Not well known at the time since he was playing in the Pacific Coast Hockey League (for the Hollywood Wolves, a Leaf farm team) at the time, Barilko quickly established himself as a strong force on the Leaf blueline. The native of Timmins, Ontario helped the Leafs to championships in 1947, 1948 and 1949. He was now very intent on adding another title to his impressive record. When Barilko reached the puck, he let a shot go using a sweeping backhand motion. The drive sailed over the shoulder of Montreal netminder Gerry McNeil for the winning goal. The clock behind the Montreal net showed it was about 10 minutes past 11:00 PM but the Toronto crowd went wild in celebration of the overtime tally that secured the Stanley Cup. It was the only time to date that the Leafs have ever won the NHL championship with an overtime goal. After the game was over, Barilko was congratulated in the dressing room by all his teammates and owner Conn Smythe who made it a special point to shake the hero's hand. As for the winning goal Barilko simply said, "It's something I've dreamed about doing all my life." Just 24 years of age at the time, Barilko was living the all-Canadian dream by starring for the Maple Leafs and winning championships for the blue and white. Sadly, that all came to an end when he went on a fishing trip to northern Ontario with a friend on a small plane in late August of 1951. The pair never made it back and their remains at the crash site were not found for 11 years—which just happened to be the next time the Leafs were champs again.

The Leafs crumbled as a team between 1952 and 1958 losing or trading away a variety of good players who had helped them win four titles. The biggest loss was the tragic demise of Barilko but he did leave a great memory for all fans of the game. The musical group The Tragically Hip wrote a song about Barilko and his famous goal, (50 Mission Cap) and that helps to keep the kid from Ontario fresh in the hearts and minds of Toronto hockey fans.

27 Greatest Goals in Maple Leafs History (Playoffs)

1. **April 9, 1932**—Ace Bailey scores game-winning goal as Leafs capture their first ever Stanley Cup on home ice with 6–4 win over the New York Rangers.

2. **April 3, 1933**—Ken Doraty scores in the sixth overtime period to defeat the Boston Bruins after 104:46 of extra play to win 1–0. The goal sends the Leafs to the Stanley Cup final.

3. **April 18, 1942**—Pete Langelle scores Game 7–winning goal versus Detroit to complete Leafs' comeback from three games down.

4. **April 21, 1951**—Bill Barilko scores Stanley Cup–winning goal in overtime.

5. **April 22, 1962**—Dick Duff scores winning goal for first Stanley Cup of the 1960s on the road versus Chicago.

6. **April 23, 1964**—Bob Baun scores overtime winner with broken bone in his leg to take sixth game in Detroit and force seventh game in Toronto.

7. **April 25, 1964**—Recently acquired Andy Bathgate scores game-winning goal in Leafs 4–0 Game 7 triumph over Detroit.

8. **April 25, 1967**—Bob Pulford scores double-overtime winner versus Rogie Vachon of Montreal to give Leafs 2–1 series lead in 1967 finals.

9. **April 29, 1978**—Lanny McDonald scores in overtime to defeat New York Islanders 2–1 in Game 7 showdown—first seven-game series win for Leafs since 1964.

10. **May 1, 1993 and May 3, 1993**—Nik Borschevsky eliminates Red Wings with overtime goal and Doug Gilmour scores overtime wraparound goal to win first game of series versus the St. Louis Blues.

28 Ten More Memorable Maple Leaf Goals (Playoffs)

1. **April 22, 1945**—Babe Pratt scores late goal to give Leafs 2–1 win at Detroit in Game 7 to capture Stanley Cup.

2. **March 31, 1959**—Frank Mahovlich scores in overtime of Game 4 versus Boston to get the Leafs back into the semi-final series.

3. **April 18, 1963**—Eddie Shack scores Cup-winning goal to defeat Red Wings 3–1 and take second straight title.

4. **April 9, 1964**—Dave Keon scores three goals in Leafs 3–1 win at the Montreal Forum to win Game 7.

5. **May 2, 1967**—Jim Pappin scores Cup-winning goal versus Montreal—his seventh of the playoffs.

6. **April 22, 1976**—Darryl Sittler scores five goals in one game versus Philadelphia at Maple Leaf Gardens against goalie Bernie Parent.

7. **May 27, 1993**—Wendel Clark scores three goals versus the Los Angeles Kings but Leafs lose 5–4 in overtime.

8. **May 17, 1999**—Gary Valk scores in overtime to eliminate Pittsburgh Penguins.

9. **April 13, 2001**—Mats Sundin scores overtime winner to beat Ottawa Senators 1–0 in series opener.

10. **May 4, 2002**—Gary Roberts scores triple overtime winner to defeat Senators and tie series 1–1.

29 Darryl Sittler

Toronto owner Harold Ballard was never one to hide his displeasure when it came to one of his star players not playing well. The 1975–76 season was no different with Ballard setting his sights on team captain Darryl Sittler. On February 6, 1976, Ballard unleashed a verbal assault on Sittler in an interview with the *Toronto Star*. Ballard told writer Frank Orr that the Maple Leafs were on the lookout for a "sensational centre" to play between wingers Lanny McDonald and Errol Thompson. "We'd set off a time bomb if we had a hell of a centre in there," Ballard bellowed in typical fashion. The clear implication was that the centre currently playing on that line (Sittler) was not nearly adequate.

The high-flying Boston Bruins (32–10–9) were coming in to play the Leafs on Saturday night, February 7th and the Don Cherry coached team was clearly the favourite for this contest. The Leafs were ready for this one and scored the first two goals of the game by McDonald and Ian Turnbull. Each of the Toronto tallies was assisted by Sittler. Boston got one back to end the first period 2–1 for Toronto. Sittler scored three times in the second period and assisted on two others and the Leafs led the game 8–4 after two periods.

The Bruins started rookie goalie Dave Reece for this game at the Gardens and while he had played well so far (including recording two shutouts), this was not going to be his night. Sittler added three more goals in the final period to give him 10 points (6G, 4A) on the night—the most ever recorded by one player in a single game. The unprecedented offensive outburst vaulted Sittler into tenth place in league scoring and gave him something he could use in response to Ballard's salvos the previous day. Named the first star of the game, Sittler was interviewed by Dave Hodge on *Hockey Night in Canada*. The post-game conversation went (in part) something like this:

Dave Hodge: Errol Thompson and Lanny McDonald are your new wingers and the line was put together to get you going, how much better were you with the new wingers?

Darryl Sittler was the Toronto captain from 1975 to 1982.
(Harold Barkley Archives)

Darryl Sittler: I give them all the credit ... when you are playing with good guys like that, they move the puck around and create openings ... Mr. Ballard probably thinks he is a hero now because this week he gave me a shot in the newspaper. He says he was looking for a good centre to play between Lanny and Errol and hopefully that would tee me off.

Dave Hodge: Jim Gregory (the Maple Leafs general manager) just congratulated you and said they want the stick for the Hall of Fame and you said (what in reply)?

Darryl Sittler: I need to keep the stick to for the next few games as we need the wins.

Dave Hodge: You know of course that hockey players don't go back to the bench and automatically count up the number of points they have at a certain point, at what time did you realize that something special was happening tonight?

Darryl Sittler: Well, I think it was when I scored my seventh point, I knew I was close to a record. Then in the dressing room Stan Obodiac, (the Leafs public relations man), told me I was closing on some (long established NHL) scoring records. It just happened to work out, my last point I just had to pass it out in front and it went into the net—just one of those things.

Dave Hodge: Darryl Sittler, thank you very much and the score 11 to 4 for the Leafs, but the biggest thing is Darryl Sittler's 10 points in one game. We bid you good night from Maple Leaf Gardens in Toronto.

It was indeed a special night for a player who had worked so hard to become a star player for the Maple Leafs as well as their team captain. Sittler would go on to have many more memorable nights in a Toronto uniform and would conclude his career with an induction into the Hockey Hall of Fame. Ballard may never have appreciated his best player but all Toronto fans still give Sittler his richly deserved recognition as one of the best Maple Leafs of all time.

30 2/7/76—The 10-Point Night

There are 10 things you should know about Darryl Sittler's 10-point night of February 7, 1976:

1. The only Maple Leaf to score a goal that Sittler wasn't involved with was George Ferguson. The Leaf centre also assisted on one of Sittler's goals.

2. Toronto defenseman Borje Salming recorded a four-point night (2G, 2A) while winger Lanny McDonald also had four-point night (1G, 3A) while Errol Thompson had three assists. Salming was named the second star of the game while McDonald was named the third.

3. Sittler's eighth point tied the mark previously established by Maurice Richard and Bert Olmstead for their performances in one game while both were members of the Montreal Canadiens. No other NHL player has posted more than eight points in one game since Sittler's magical night.

4. The Leafs had a rare Sunday night home game on February 8th and beat Minnesota 4–1 with Sittler getting one assist.

5. Boston rookie netminder Dave Reece (a native of Troy, New York) came into the game with a 7–4–2 mark but never played in the NHL after the 11–4 loss in Toronto.

6. Gerry Cheevers was just back in a Boston uniform from his time in the WHA and was on the Bruins bench but wanted no part of going in to relieve Reece. The Bruins beat Detroit 7–0 the next night in Boston with Cheevers in net.

7. Boston star Jean Ratelle scored his 350th career goal in the same game as Sittler's 10 points.

8. Don Cherry claims the Bruins never lost in Toronto while he was coaching Boston after Sittler's great night—not true

according to the scoring summaries. The Bruins were pretty good however posting a 7–2–2 record between 1976 and 1979 at Maple Leaf Gardens, with Cherry behind the Bruin's bench.

9. Harold Ballard later gave Sittler a silver tea service to mark his great achievement.

10. Sittler's great game is captured in a children's book entitled *My Leafs Sweater* by Mike Leonetti.

31 2/2/77—Ian Turnbull's Five-Goal Night

Ten things you should know about Ian Turnbull's five-goal night of February 2, 1977, during a 9–1 win over Detroit:

1. Turnbull had not scored a goal in the previous 30 games but his five-goal effort raised his season total from 11 to 16.

2. Turnbull scored on all five shots he took in the game.

3. Leaf defenseman Borje Salming set up three of Turnbull's goals including the last one with a picture-perfect pass right up the middle of the ice. It was scored at the 18:30 mark of the final period.

4. Two of Turnbull's goals were unassisted.

5. Hall of Fame netminder Eddie Giacomin gave up the first two Turnbull goals for Detroit while Jimmy Rutherford gave up the other three.

6. The Red Wings coach that night was Larry Wilson. His son Ron would go on to play for and coach the Maple Leafs in the future.

7. Turnbull took a minor penalty in the third period of the game but that did not stop him from scoring three times in the final frame.

Defenseman Ian Turnbull scored five goals during a 9–1 win over Detroit on February 2, 1977. (Robert Shaver)

8. Leaf captain Darryl Sittler did not play in this game but Turnbull was given a silver tea service by owner Harold Ballard just like he had given to Sittler in recognition of his great 10-point performance.
9. Turnbull broke the mark for most goals by a Leaf defenseman in one game—previously set by Hap Day who scored four times in one game versus Pittsburgh in 1929.
10. Turnbull would score four goals in one game for the Kings on December 12, 1981 after he was traded to the Kings by the Maple Leafs just one-month prior on November 11, 1981.

32 Paul Henderson

When the Maple Leafs acquired left winger Paul Henderson in the trade that saw Toronto legend Frank Mahovlich go to Detroit in March of 1968, they knew they had one of the fastest players in the league on their team. Toronto coach and general manager Punch Imlach vowed he would get the speedy Henderson for his Leafs one day and kept good on his word when he made the blockbuster trade. The Leafs also got one of the steadiest performers in the game and a player who could score 25 to 30 goals with ease most seasons. What the Leafs did not know was that they had secured the rights to a performer who would go on to become a national icon.

Henderson was generally a good to very good player most nights but could also be a star on more than one occasion. A four-goal game while with the Red Wings was proof of that, as was his 38-goal season in 1971–72 which placed him tenth in league scoring that year. His excellent performance earned him an invite to the 1972 Team Canada training camp where a large group of

NHL players were preparing to meet the Soviet Union for an eight-game series to be played in September of '72. Nobody expected the Russians to make it much of a series and fewer expected Henderson to be a major factor, but the experts were all wrong.

Paul Henderson scored three game winners for Team Canada in the 1972 Summit Series. (*Toronto Star*)

Playing on a line with Bobby Clarke and Toronto teammate Ron Ellis, Henderson recorded 10 points (7G, 3A) while scoring the last three game-winning goals as Canada eked out a 4–3–1 series win. His game winner in the seventh game was a spectacular individual effort and that tally led to the final game being the series-deciding contest. Henderson's last game winner game came with 34 seconds to play and secured a 6–5 win for the Canadian side in the final contest of the series. His determination to score made sure the Canadian efforts to get back into the series (after being down 1–2–1 in the four games played in Canada) did not go to waste. To be sure it was a great team effort and 15 players on the Canadian roster would go into the Hall of Fame along with coach Harry Sinden. The question is should there be one more—namely Paul Henderson.

Although he never advocates for himself, the question has always been raised after Russian netminder Vladislav Tretiak was inducted in to the Hall in 1989. How can the goalie Henderson beat for his dramatic three game winners be in the hallowed Hall and he is left out? Many will point to Henderson's career numbers as not being overwhelming and while that may be true, he recorded 477 points in the NHL and then another 283 in the WHA after he left the Maple Leafs. Perhaps if all his points were earned in the NHL it might be a different story, but he did play in over 1,000 professional games before retiring.

Henderson also had a very strong junior career with the Hamilton Red Wings (a Memorial Cup win in 1962 plus a 49-goal season) and was elected to play in the NHL All-Star game twice. He had 20 or more goals in seven of his NHL seasons and had 30 or more twice—both while playing in Toronto. He led the entire NHL in game winning goals one year, nine in 1965–66 and in 1966–67 he had the most short-handed goals with seven. Henderson played in the Stanley Cup final on two occasions (both with Detroit in 1964 and 1966). He was always among the top point producers on every team he played and was one of the best performers on Team Canada '72, competing strongly with some of the best players in the game. Henderson's mark on the "Series of the Century" is indelible and the photo of his winning goal is forever etched into Canadian sports history. He is also one of the most sportsmanlike players to have performed at a high level in the NHL and is considered a great role model for young and old.

It is wonderful to note that Henderson is in the Canadian Sports Hall of Fame (in 1995) and was named to the International Ice Hockey Federation Hockey Hall of Fame (in 2013) with Paul attending the induction ceremony in Stockholm, Sweden. While those honours are well deserved it will be an injustice if Henderson does not take his rightful place in the Hockey Hall of Fame in Toronto.

33 Ten More Memorable Maple Leaf Goals (Playoffs)

1. **Paul Henderson**—If Vladislav Tretiak is in the Hall of Fame, why not Henderson, who beat him three times when it mattered most in 1972 for "Canada's Team of the Century." Don't listen to those who say he didn't have a good enough NHL career—he did!
2. **Lorne Chabot**—Won two Stanley Cups and posted 71 shutouts and 201 career victories.
3. **Alex Mogilny**—473 career goals, including over 50 tallies twice, and a two-time second-team All-Star. Dangerous player who scored 76 goals one year.

4. **Curtis Joseph**—454 career victories ranks him seventh all-time. Chosen for the 1996 World Cup and 2002 Canadian Olympic teams.

5. **Carl Brewer**—Highly skilled defenseman would have made the Hall as a player if he had played straight through. But more impactfully, he helped lead the charge for players getting their full pension benefits. He also exposed corruption in the hierarchy of the Players' Association.

34 Walter "Turk" Broda

The Maple Leafs made it to the Stanley Cup final in 1936 and their opponents were the Detroit Red Wings. The two teams were evenly matched with the Red Wings winning 24 regular season games, good for first place in the American Division of the NHL while the Maple Leafs had won 23, good for second place in the Canadian Division. The Leafs beat the Boston Bruins and the New York Americans to reach the final while the Red Wings beat the Montreal Maroons to advance to the best-of-five final.

The final did not go well for the Maple Leafs who dropped the first two games of the series by 3–1 and 9–4 scores. Toronto general manager Conn Smythe was at the second game of the series played in Detroit on April 7, 1936 and agreed with many observers that Maple Leaf goaltender George Hainsworth did not look very good in net. It was suggested to Smythe that the 40-year-old Hainsworth should be replaced immediately if the Leafs were to have any chance to come back. Smythe refused to embarrass his veteran goalie who had enjoyed a stellar NHL career to this point. However, Smythe realized Hainsworth was near the end of his career and he had a chance to scout a Red Wing minor league goalie named Earl Robertson the very next night in Windsor, Ontario. Rather than return home to Toronto right away Smythe stayed behind to watch Robertson in a playoff game.

Robertson was the most highly rated goalie not in the NHL at the time but on the night of April 7, 1936, he allowed eight goals with the Windsor team going down to an 8–1 loss. Smythe sat right behind Robertson for most of the night and could not have been too impressed with his efforts, but the goalie playing for the other team definitely caught his eye. Walter Broda, a 5'9", 180-pound

Walter "Turk" Broda (left) with Ted Kennedy. (Harold Barkley Archives)

netminder had played very well for the Detroit Olympics in 1935–36 (posting a 26–18–3 record), and Smythe liked what he saw of the 21-year-old they nicknamed "Turk." Smythe said little about what he had just witnessed and he was told to ignore Robertson's bad night. However, when Smythe approached the Red Wings about buying the rights to a goalie, he did not ask for Robertson. Instead he asked for Broda and it was agreed that the price would be $8,000 to acquire the netminder. Detroit management (including general manager Jack Adams) really liked Broda but felt there was no way he could beat out 28-year-old Norm Smith who had just won them the Stanley Cup. The deal was agreed to and the Leafs secured the goalie who would guard their net from 1936 to 1951.

It might have been possible that Smythe had some prior information on Broda prior to seeing him in a game but the Leaf manager had always displayed a sharp eye for young talent and in Broda's case he was exactly right. Broda would take the Leafs to five Stanley Cups while posting a club record 302 career victories. He played in 629 career games and registered 62 career shutouts—all for the Maple Leafs. He was known as a "money goalie" and won 60 of 101 playoff appearances. The Leafs certainly got the most out of Smythe's one-night scouting trip!

As for Robertson, he would go on to play in 190 NHL games for the New York Americans and put up a 60–95–34 record while playing for a pretty bad team. Before he joined the Americans, Robertson did help Detroit win the Stanley Cup in 1937 but otherwise his career was uneventful. Broda would go on to be elected to the Hockey Hall of Fame and then coached the junior Toronto Marlies to the Memorial Cup in 1955 and 1956.

35 Syl Apps and Dave Schriner

Depending on which source you believe, Doris Klein was a young lady of about 14 years of age in 1942 who either was from Toronto or from the Detroit area. Why is she important? The Leafs were getting embarrassed in the '42 Stanley Cup final and Klein, a steadfast Toronto hockey fan, was hearing it from her friends at school about how her team was getting torn apart by the Detroit Red Wings. With the Leafs seemingly down and out, Klein wrote a letter to the team outlining her disappointment and the treatment she was receiving from those around her. She implored the team to play better and beat the Red Wings.

Klein's letter was passed on to Leafs coach Hap Day who read it to the team in the dressing room before the start of the fourth game in Detroit. After he was done Toronto forward Dave "Sweeney" Schriner stood up and said something along the lines of, "Tell that girl not to worry, we're going to come back and win it for her." With the Maple Leafs down 3–0 in games (losing the first two at Maple Leaf Gardens), Day decided to make drastic lineup changes (dropping unproductive regulars like forward Gord Drillon and defenseman Bucko McDonald) while altering how the Toronto club was going to play the rest of the series, like focusing more on dumping the puck into the Detroit end of the rink and chasing it down. By some magic, it all worked and the Leafs staged a historic rally that has never been matched. Klein and her father were also offered tickets to a game as guests of the Maple Leafs and her photo appeared in a Toronto newspaper.

Led by captain Syl Apps who scored an important goal, the Leafs won the fourth game in Detroit by a 4–3 score before returning home to whip the Red Wings 9–3. The Detroit club was

Syl Apps with the 1942 Stanley Cup. (City of Toronto Archives)

now desperate to end the series at home for the sixth contest but Toronto goalie Turk Broda would not allow a single Red Wing tally in a 3–0 Leafs win. The Leafs were ready to play the Saturday night contest on April 18, 1942 when the seventh and deciding game was played at the Gardens. But it was by no means easy.

Detroit opened the scoring and it stayed 1–0 until the third period when the inspired Schriner tied it up. "I didn't know I had scored until I heard the crowd shouting and then I saw the (red) light go on. It was the biggest light I ever saw in my life," said Schriner after the game about his first goal. Pete Langelle gave the Leafs the lead and Schriner scored another to make it a 3–1 final before a record crowd (at the time) of 16,218 delirious Maple Leaf fans. The Stanley Cup was presented to captain Apps (who finished the final with seven points) who then gave it to Maple Leafs manager Conn Smythe in attendance despite his World War II army duties.

It is of course very difficult to determine just how much Klein's letter inspired the Maple Leafs. The Toronto club was clearly superior (57 regular season points compared to just 42) to the Detroit team so maybe it was just a matter of time before the Maple Leafs took over, but if there was a point where the Leafs turned it around, it may have been spurred on by the letter. The Leafs also took the time to acknowledge Klein publicly and that says something about what the team thought about her efforts. Years later there were stories that other such letters were received by the team, but only Klein's prose was made known and for that she holds a special place in team history for her helping the club secure the '42 Stanley Cup—the first championship in a decade for the Maple Leafs. It should also be noted that no other professional sports team since the '42 Maple Leafs has ever come back to win the final series that decides the ultimate champion for the season!

36 Top 10 Maple Leaf Teams of All Time

1. **1931–32**—First Toronto team to play in Maple Leaf Gardens while finishing second in Canadian Division before sweeping New York Rangers 3–0 in the Stanley Cup final.

2. **1941–42**—Leaf team comes back from 3–0 deficit in Cup final to beat Detroit in seven games.

3. **1946–47**—Leafs post a 31–19–10 regular season record for a second-place finish and wins over Montreal in the finals for the Stanley Cup.

4. **1947–48**—Leafs finish first overall during the regular season and win the Stanley Cup in just nine games. Conn Smythe said this was his greatest team.

5. **1948–49**—Fourth place regular season finish but Leafs win their third straight Stanley Cup (first NHL team to do so) with series wins over Boston and Detroit.

6. **1950–51**—Leafs' record 95 points in regular season, then beat Boston and Montreal to take Stanley Cup.

7. **1961–62**—This Toronto team wins Stanley Cup for the first time in 11 years and brings respectability back to the Maple Leafs.

8. **1962–63**—Leafs finish first overall during regular season with 82 points and lose just two games in the playoffs on the way to the Stanley Cup title.

9. **1963–64**—Gritty Leafs survive average season but win their third straight Stanley Cup winning two seven-games series versus Montreal and Detroit.

10. **1966–67**—Up-and-down season features a veteran team that finishes third but brings it all together in the playoffs, beating Chicago and Montreal to take Stanley Cup.

37 Top Five Leaf Teams That Didn't Win the Cup

1. 1960–61—Recorded 90 points with a 39–19–12 record. Leafs were hampered with injuries and were upset in semi-final playoff series by Detroit.
2. 1977–78—Leafs win 41 games in regular season under coach Roger Neilson and upset New York Islanders in playoffs but then get swept by Montreal Canadiens in the semi-finals.
3. 1992–93—Leafs record 44 wins in regular season and make a surprising run in playoffs only to lose Western Conference final to Wayne Gretzky and the Los Angeles Kings.
4. 1993–94—Leafs win 43 games and record 98 points but lose Western Conference final once again—this time to Vancouver.
5. 2001–02—Leafs record 100 points in regular season—the second-best mark in the Eastern Conference and third best overall—but lose to Carolina in third round of playoffs.

38 Gerry James

A native of Regina, Saskatchewan, Gerry James was one of the most versatile athletes in the history of Canadian professional sports. His first claim to fame was as a star running back in the Canadian Football League with the Winnipeg Blue Bombers. James began his football career when he was just 17 years old in 1952 and by 1954, he was named the outstanding Canadian player. Part of a powerful Bomber backfield, James helped the Winnipeg team to the Grey

Cup game on six occasions and was on the winning side four times. James scored 19 touchdowns in 1957 with 18 of the scores coming on the ground and established a new CFL record that would last until 1981 when it was matched.

Considering he was such a prolific football player; it was a wonder that James would do anything that might jeopardize his gridiron career but the CFL never paid much. When he was given a chance to pursue a hockey career, he jumped at the chance to join the Maple Leafs who owned his rights. Once the football season was over in 1954, James came to Toronto to join the junior Marlboros and was on the team that captured the Memorial Cup for the 1954–55 season. The Marlies team he played on featured future Maple Leafs like Billy Harris, Bob Pulford, Bob Nevin and Mike Nykoluk. James also got into one Leaf game that season.

James did not star in hockey as he did in football but he was a nice utility player for the Maple Leafs who could check with some gusto and also kill penalties. He played in 46 games for Toronto in 1955–56 and scored his first NHL goal versus the Detroit Red Wings on March 3, 1956 at Maple Leaf Gardens. James put in a rebound of a Sid Smith shot over the body of Red Wings net-minder Glenn Hall. The Leafs struggled to finish fourth in '55–'56 (with only 24 wins), but James still made his presence known. He caught the eye of Conn Smythe, the longtime Leaf owner who had seen many great hockey players in his time. "Gerry James is one of the greatest athletes I've ever seen. Our club was lying down dead until he joined us at the end of the football season," commented Smythe.

James would play in 53 games for the Leafs in 1956–57 and scored four goals, totaling a career best 16 points to go along with 90 penalty minutes. He divided the 1957–58 season between Toronto and Rochester of the AHL but returned to the Maple Leafs for the 1959–60 season, which saw him play in the Stanley

Cup final for the first time. This was after he had played in the 1959 Grey Cup game for the Bombers (defeating the Hamilton Tiger-Cats), and he made history by being the only man to play in both the CFL and NHL final (the Leafs lost the Stanley Cup final to the Montreal Canadiens) in the same season. He was put on a line with Garry "Duke" Edmundson and Johnny Wilson, and coach Punch Imlach would send the line out when he needed to stir things up. His 10 appearances in the 1960 playoffs were his final games as a Maple Leaf finishing with 40 points in 149 regular season games.

James played one football season in Saskatchewan before returning to hockey at the minor league level for four seasons and played until he was 37 years old. He then turned to coaching to stay in sports but as great an athlete as James was in his era, he never made the kind of money that later day two-sport stars (like Deion Sanders and Bo Jackson who both excelled at baseball and football) earned in the modern times. Gerry James' name should be brought up more often when great Canadian athletes are discussed.

39 Miscalculations by Toronto Maple Leafs Management

1. Missing Out on Bobby Orr

On March 28, 1960, Leaf coach Punch Imlach received a letter from a Pee Wee coach in Parry Sound who suggested that a 12-year-old boy named Bobby Orr was worth putting on the Leafs' protected list before another NHL team did. The Leaf organization failed to act on the tip. The rest is history.

2. Stripping Their Farm System

In 1966, the Leaf owners sold their top minor league team, the Rochester Americans for cash and then a year later peddled their Victoria farm team. The 1967 Expansion draft further depleted their player depth. It took the organization years to recover.

3. Not Taking the World Hockey Association More Seriously

After finishing last in the Eastern Division after the 1969–70 season, Leaf General Manager Jim Gregory rebuilt the team with good young players and amazingly pilfered goalie Bernie Parent from the Flyers. The result was playoff hockey in both 1970–71 and 1971–72. The Leafs lost in the 1972 quarter-finals in 5 games to the powerful Bruins who went on to win the Stanley Cup. But there was much optimism that the team with a combination of veterans like Dave Keon, Norm Ullman, Jacques Plante and younger players such as Parent, Darryl Sittler, Rick Kehoe, Rick Ley and others would be able to challenge Boston and Montreal for the championship in the coming years.

However, the advent of the World Hockey Association in 1972–73 put a stop to any progress made. The Leafs lost many players to the upstart league including future Hall of Famer Bernie Parent, defensemen Rick Ley and Brad Selwood and tough centreman Jim Harrison. Paul Henderson and Dave Keon would also leave soon. Consequently, the Leafs missed the playoffs that season with one of the worst teams in their history.

Teams like the New York Rangers decided to increase their payroll and keep their star players but Harold Ballard did not believe the new league would last and wouldn't and/or couldn't retain the players.

4. Upper Management Kept General Manager John Ferguson Jr. Far Too Long

Richard Peddie hired John Ferguson Jr. prior to the start of the 2003-04 season and the Leafs made the playoffs that season with a team built by the previous general manager Pat Quinn. The team missed the playoffs the next two seasons and in January of 2008 with the Leafs in 28th place in the overall standings, Ferguson was released from his duties. The ill-advised trades including high draft picks, poor free agent signings as well as the several no trade contracts given out affected the team adversely going forward as the Leafs missed the playoffs again in the 2007–08 season and failed to make the post-season the next four years. When a general manager starts making moves to protect his own job and not necessarily for the benefit of his organization, then it's time for upper management to make a move. That move took far too long.

5. "Draft Schmaft"—Trading of Draft Picks

Cliff Fletcher was once rated as a first-rate General Manager having won a Stanley Cup in Calgary in 1989 and reviving the Leaf fortunes with outstanding trades, especially obtaining Doug Gilmour. Leafs made it to the final four in both the 1992–93 and 1993–94 seasons but the magic eventually wore off and after three underachieving seasons, Fletcher was let go after the 1996–97 season. After John Ferguson Jr. was fired in January of 2008, Fletcher was asked to return on an 'interim' basis. But his 'Draft Schmaft' view of building a team proceeded to dig the Leafs into a deeper hole. The trading of future draft picks along with the questionable trade of Alex Steen and Carlo Colaiacovo for Lee Stempniak just made the rebuild tougher for the incoming GM Brian Burke.

40 Five Worst Maple Leaf Teams of All Time

1. 1957–58—Leafs sink to the bottom of the NHL to finish sixth overall for the first time under the leadership of the Smythe family.
2. 1969–70—Just three seasons removed from the Stanley Cup triumph of 1967, the Leafs finish last in the East Division.
3. 1972–73—Toronto owner Harold Ballard spends the season incarcerated while the Maple Leafs finish dead last in the East Division with just 27 wins after losing several players to the new league—the WHA.
4. 1981–82—Leafs set a franchise record for fewest wins in one season 20 (during 82-game regular season).
5. 1984–85—Leafs finish with just 20 wins and are the worst team in hockey, giving them the first pick of the 1985 NHL Entry Draft.

41 Bob Pulford

Prior to the start of the 1963–64 season there was only one penalty box in each of the six NHL arenas. That meant players who had a fight with an opponent would have to sit next to him once it was over with maybe a police officer sitting between them. It was not always ideal but spectator seats along the boards were precious and owners did not want to lose any revenue by expanding penalty boxes when one seating area would do. But it did not always work well when tempers flared and there were cases where the trouble continued in the box.

One such occasion was on October 30, 1963 when the Montreal Canadiens paid a visit to Maple Leaf Gardens. The Maple Leafs went up 2–0 in the first period on a pair of goals by Eddie Litzenberger but there was trouble early in the second stanza. Montreal defenseman Terry Harper was caught high-sticking Toronto centre Bob Pulford. The burly Leaf pivot did not take kindly to the assault and gave the stick back to Harper before they engaged in a fight. It looked like things had calmed down when the two went to the penalty box, but Pulford decided it was not over and launched another attack on Harper while the pair were sitting in the box. NHL president Clarence Campbell was seated next to the penalty box and got a great view of the action. Both players earned 10-minute misconducts for the melee in the box but neither was tossed from the game.

Pulford's performance in this game (a 6–3 Toronto victory) was typical of the way the two-way centre played his entire career as a Maple Leaf. In addition to his combative play against the Canadiens that night, Pulford scored once and added two assists. Pulford was most often around the 20-goal mark every season (he scored a career high 28 goals in 1965–66) and could play any role asked of him even though he did not have the skill level of Dave Keon and Red Kelly who also played centre for the Maple Leafs in the 1960s. His feisty nature made him a great checker but he could always score key goals including 25 career tallies in the playoffs. Pulford was elected to the Hall of Fame in 1991.

"He hit me with his stick," Pulford complained afterward about his encounter with Harper. "I don't know if it was intentional but you know how it is, you lose your temper." Harper said his stick was up because Pulford had his up high as well. "He (Pulford) hit me in the penalty box while I was sitting down. I was surprised...But he was pretty mad." The incident was not lost on

Bob Pulford (#20) checks Montreal captain Jean Beliveau in front of goalie Bruce Gamble. (York University Archives/*Toronto Telegram* Collection)

Leaf president Stafford Smythe who made the case for separate boxes: "It's ridiculous to ask two guys who've been trying to knock each other's heads off to sit quietly side by side." Smythe vowed to add another penalty box during the '63–'64 season provided some logistical problems could be worked out. The fight (plus an injury to Montreal netminder Gump Worsley) helped to delay the game significantly so the NHL had an interest in resolving the problem as well.

On November 8, 1963, the Gardens implemented two penalty boxes for the game between Toronto and Chicago. The boxes were put to good use on this night with 27 penalties called during the game with 14 going to the Maple Leafs during the 3–3 tie with the Black Hawks. No matter the outcome, hockey history was made with two separate penalty boxes, an innovation that was here to stay.

42 Ten Hockey Innovations Started at Maple Leaf Gardens

1. **Separate penalty boxes**—Necessary to stop brawls from continuing in the penalty box.
2. **Time clocks with four faces**—Everyone in the building could now get a look at the game clock.
3. **Painting the ice white**—Made for a much better appearance than the dull grey look. Much more appealing when television arrived.
4. **Herculite glass above boards**—Shatterproof glass became a necessity as players started shooting the puck harder and higher.
5. **Red Lights**—Placed behind each net and let everyone know the puck had crossed the goal line.
6. **Goal Judges**—While sitting behind the goals, the judges push the red light for a goal and help out the referee.
7. **Escalators**—Most of the early buildings only had stairwells for fans to climb to the upper balconies and seats, but escalators allowed for quicker and more efficient movement of fans.
8. **Clocking of ice time**—The amount of time spent on the ice by each player was recorded using a wall of clocks. Time on ice is tracked more today than ever.

9. **Hand barrels**—Filled with water, these were the first to provide a fresh flood between periods—a job now done by the Zamboni.
10. **First televised game**—March 21, 1951, vs. Montreal as an in-house production for CBC employees to prepare for the start of *Hockey Night in Canada* in 1952.

43 Peter Stemkowski

For most of the decade of the 1960s the Boston Bruins were not a very good team. Mired in the basement of the NHL between 1960 and 1967, the Bruins struggled to win every night of the year despite some decent talent at the forward position. Johnny Bucyk, Murray Oliver, Tom Williams, Dean Prentice and Andy Hebenton provided some scoring while Ted Green, Ed Westfall and Don Awrey gave some hope along the blueline along with Ed Johnston in goal. The 1963–64 season was not a good one for the Bruins who won just 18 of 70 games and recorded a total of 48 points. However, on the night of January 18, 1964, the Bruins shocked the Maple Leafs on Toronto's home ice to the tune of an 11–0 shellacking of the defending Stanley Cup champions!

The onslaught started early and lasted all game long. Youngster Gary Dornhoefer scored 53 seconds into the game when he beat Leaf netminder Don Simmons. Hebenton scored twice as did Prentice while Oliver added a single to make it 6–0 by the first intermission. One more goal in the second made it 7–0 before four more Boston tallies made the final 11–0. Johnston turned aside 26 Leaf shots that were rather feeble efforts on this night. The crowd at the Gardens started to cheer the Bruins while taking out their unhappiness on the hometown Maple Leafs.

The Toronto lineup featured one rookie making his NHL debut and he managed to get on the scoresheet by serving a bench minor. Centre Peter Stemkowski was called up for the game from the OHA leading junior Toronto Marlboros. Stemkowski recorded 103 points (including 42 goals) in the '63–'64 season for the Memorial Cup winning Marlies, but never got called back to

Peter Stemkowski (#12) watches Bobby Orr (#5) during the 1968 All-Star game. (Harold Barkley Archives)

the Leafs for the rest of the year, which saw the Leafs rally to take their third straight championship. The burly (6'1", 196 pounds) pivot split the next season between Toronto and Rochester of the American Hockey League before staying with the Leafs full time in 1965–66. He had his best year as a Maple Leaf in 1966–67 when he recorded 35 points in 68 games played and saved his best for the '67 playoffs with 12 points in 12 games. He centered the Leafs most consistent line in the playoffs with Bob Pulford and Jim Pappin on the wings. It was quite the turnaround for Stemkowski considering how his NHL career had started in that now infamous game against the Bruins!

The 1967–68 season was a difficult one in Toronto and the 24-year-old Stemkowski was dealt to Detroit in the deal that saw Frank Mahovlich also go to the Red Wings. In that blockbuster deal the Leafs also gave up another promising centre in 20-year-old Garry Unger and threw in the rights to retired star defenseman Carl Brewer in the deal. The Leafs did get two quality players in the transaction (Norm Ullman and Paul Henderson), but not much else considering all they had turned over to Detroit. Keeping Stemkowski and/or Unger might have made the Leafs an entirely different team going forward, but Leafs general manager and coach Punch Imlach was determined to move Mahovlich at any price and they paid dearly for this transaction as the years passed.

Stemkowski would go on to play in 967 NHL games and record 555 points (including 209 goals). Unger set an NHL record by playing in 914 consecutive games (since broken) while recording 804 points (including 413 goals) in 1,105 total games. These are great totals from two players the Leafs could have surely used as they tried to rebuild from their Stanley Cup years of the 1960s.

44 Bob Baun

When the Maple Leafs won the Stanley Cup in 1963, they did so with an easy romp in the playoffs. The first place Toronto club eliminated the Montreal Canadiens in just five games and then did the same to the Detroit Red Wings in the final. Many felt the Leafs could have taken the Cup in eight straight games but both Montreal and Detroit did their best to not lose the last game of their season on home ice.

The 1964 playoffs were quite a different story. The Maple Leafs ultimately prevailed to take their third straight championship, but it was a difficult path to the title. Montreal was the first-round opposition but this time it took the Leafs seven games to oust the first place Canadiens and they had to win the final two games of the series to advance to the final once again. The Red Wings proved to be a much more difficult challenge in the '64 postseason and the teams split the first four games of the series. When Detroit won the fifth game of the series at Maple Leaf Gardens, it gave the Red Wings the opportunity to win the Stanley Cup on home ice the night of April 23, 1964. The contest played that night would go down as one of the most famous playoff games of all time.

The Leafs started the game well on a short-handed goal by Bob Pulford but soon found themselves down 2–1. Pulford tied it up with another tally but Detroit great Gordie Howe beat Leaf netminder Johnny Bower to give the Red Wings a 3–2 lead. Toronto tied it at 3–3 when Billy Harris knocked one past Terry Sawchuk in the Red Wings' net before the end of the second period. The score remained tied right through to the end of the regulation time.

During the third period Toronto defenseman Bob Baun took a shot on the ankle and had to be stretchered off the ice. After consulting with two doctors, it was agreed that Baun could not do any more damage to his lower limb if he went back to play. His lower leg was tightly bandaged and he was given a shot of painkiller. He returned to the ice for the final few minutes of play in the third and was also at his usual post when overtime began. Very early in the extra session, the Leafs threw the puck into the Red Wings' end and the speedy Dave Keon chased down Detroit defenseman Al Langlois. Knowing that Keon was right on him, Langlois ringed the puck along the boards hoping to clear the Detroit zone.

However, Baun was at the point and trapped the puck at the blueline. He let a shot go that hit the stick of Detroit defenseman Bill Gadsby and it floated over the shoulder of Sawchuk for the winning goal. The 4–3 victory at the Detroit Olympia kept the Leafs' hopes alive for the third consecutive title and nobody was happier than Baun, even though he was in agony once the pain-killer wore off. With a day off between the last two games of the series, Baun made himself scarce (refusing to have an x-ray taken) and showed up on Saturday night for the seventh and deciding game. He was chided in warm-ups by Gadsby and Detroit coach Sid Abel who simply did not believe Baun was that badly injured. With his injured foot taped and frozen once again, Baun played the entire game as the Maple Leafs won 4–0. It was later revealed Baun had a small broken bone in his foot.

Baun's heroic tally in the sixth game is one of the most revered goals in hockey history and it should be considering the pain he must have endured to just get back out on the ice. But there were other Leaf heroes to consider from the '64 championship squad. Defenseman Carl Brewer was playing with a rib separation that kept him out of the first two games of the series. By the last two games he was one of the best Leafs on the ice and was particularly outstanding in the sixth game in Detroit. Captain George Armstrong had a bad shoulder throughout the final series yet he managed to score a goal in the final game.

Bob Baun checks Chicago's Eric Nesterenko (#15). (Harold Barkley Archives)

Centre Red Kelly took a bad hit to the knee (delivered by Gadsby) in the sixth game played in Detroit and had strained ligaments to contend with for the final game. Like all the other injured Maple Leafs, Kelly took a shot of the painkiller Novocaine and went out for the final game of the series. He also scored one of the Toronto goals in the third period and then collapsed in the dressing room before being rushed to the hospital. It takes a total team effort to win the Stanley Cup and the '64 champs are proof that players with great character do whatever it takes to win.

Bob Baun may be the most celebrated hero of the '64 Stanley Cup winning team but others like Brewer, Armstrong, and Kelly deserve mention when great determined efforts are discussed about a team that did everything, they could to win a third straight title.

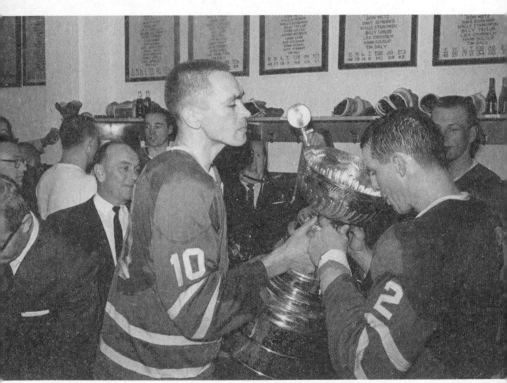

George Armstrong gives Carl Brewer a sip from the 1964 Stanley Cup.
(York University Archives/*Toronto Telegram* Collection)

45 The Chum Witch

Toronto goalie Johnny Bower turned 39 years of age during the 1963–64 season with the Maple Leafs hoping to capture their third straight Stanley Cup. The goalie known as the "China Wall" was definitely slowing down with injuries limiting his season to 51 games played, although he did have a winning record of 24–16–11. It was also not an easy season for the Leafs who finished third with 78 points and were troubled by a lack of goal scoring at times. However, late in the season the Leafs received a boost with a trade they made with New York which got them veterans Andy Bathgate and Don McKenney. Then they got an added bonus in the form of a locally created "witch."

On February 13 1964 while commenting on a particularly awful Leafs loss the night before (4–0 to the Canadiens), a news reader at 1050 CHUM Radio (on the AM dial) in Toronto commented, "The Maple Leafs lost another one last night. Maybe they need a CHUM witch to put a spell on their opponents." With that announcement, "Mabel Leaf" the CHUM Witch, was born. Dressed in black with a pointed hat and some awful green makeup, she looked very much like the Wicked Witch of the West, but in reality, she was really lounge singer Phyllis Shea in disguise. She started out stirring a steaming brew on Carlton Street outside the Gardens' entrance before the game on February 15th. Just before the opening face-off, Mabel Leaf made her way to the Blues section of Maple Leaf Gardens (CHUM's corporate seats), and waved her wand as she spewed out hexes on the Chicago Black Hawks. That night, Toronto won 4–0. The Chum Witch would go on to brew up a very impressive record of 11–2–1 over the regular season and had some magic left over for the playoffs. The city of Toronto was somewhat enthralled with the CHUM Witch (especially the ever superstitious Leafs coach Punch Imlach who insisted on the witch's attendance at home games) and she even made the cover of the CHUM Chart which listed the top 50 songs of the day (the Beatles held six of the top 10 positions for the week of March 9, 1964).

The Leafs finished the year strongly (six wins in the month of March) but struggled to beat Montreal in seven games during the semi-finals. Bower was being written off by the media, but he beat Montreal the last two games of the series, allowing only one goal during those contests. Detroit had the Maple Leafs on the ropes in the final series but Bower once again pulled out wins in Game 6 and 7 (which was a 4–0 shutout) to win the Cup once more. The CHUM Witch (who by now had two assistants) was prominent throughout the playoffs and certainly for the seventh contest at the

The CHUM Chart was a weekly ranking of the Top 30 songs in Toronto. In 1964, The Beatles ruled, except for the playoffs, when the CHUM Witch graced the cover and made the phenomenon of "hexing" the opposition to help the Leafs win the Stanley Cup one of the best radio promotions of the era.
(Courtesy of the CHUM Group)

Gardens against Detroit. Her presence and influence did not go unnoticed by Bower.

The Leaf netminder addressed the fans in the Gardens and those watching on TV after the game was over. "I'd like to thank the people of Toronto for having such patience with us. I know we did have a few bad games. And thanks very much to the CHUM Witch tonight by the way also. It is certainly wonderful to win the Stanley Cup…The city of Toronto deserves the Stanley Cup more than anybody else!" Bower may have been looking for a physiological edge as the 1963-64 season wore on and he seemed to find it with the efforts of the CHUM Witch. Bower was in net for all eight Maple Leaf playoff victories.

During the 1966–67 season Bower once again defied all the experts and helped the Leafs to their fourth championship of the decade with two superlative efforts in the Stanley Cup final versus Montreal at the ripe old age of 42—this time with no assistance from the CHUM Witch!

46 Eddie Shack

Left winger Eddie Shack was pretty miserable when he played for the New York Rangers. Shack joined the Rangers in 1958–59 after a good junior career in Guelph in the Ranger system. Even though the New York club liked Shack's potential, the native of Sudbury, Ontario could not seem to find a comfortable spot on the team and he hated coach Phil Watson. Early in the 1960–61 season it was fairly clear Shack needed a change of scenery. The Leafs offered veterans Pat Hannigan and Johnny Wilson in exchange and Shack soon became a crowd favourite in Toronto.

Shack's style of play could be best described as unpredictable yet he could be very effective in keeping the opposition on their toes. He would score just enough to keep his spot on the roster and he was able to temper his wild approach to keep coach Punch Imlach content. Sometimes his goals would be very timely as was evidenced on the night of April 18, 1963 when Shack tipped in a blueline drive to score the Stanley Cup winning goal. "I guess hard work pays off," Shack said of his important goal. "I was working hard in that last game. Kent Douglas shot the puck from the point. I got my stick on it and the puck went past Terry Sawchuk (the Detroit netminder)." The 1962–63 season had seen Shack score 16 times and his rough play earned him 97 penalty minutes. He was now an established NHL player.

In 1965–66 Shack scored a career best 26 goals during the regular season (even though he had started the year in the minors), but that was not the only interesting development for the ever colourful Maple Leaf. Shack had become so popular by this point that someone decided to write a song about him. Television broadcaster Brian McFarlane co-wrote the song along with his brother-in-law Bill McCauley. Shack was approached and gave his verbal consent so McFarlane wrote the words and McCauley penned the music.

Doug Rankine and the Secrets performed the song. Just 17 years of age at the time Rankine and the group agreed to record the song for $500. They recorded the song in just two or three takes and a number one hit was born. Side A of the 45-rpm disk was entitled, "Clear the Track, Here Comes Shack," and was released in February of 1966 on the RCA label. The song was played on *Hockey Night in Canada* with a video of Shack performing his on-ice antics which naturally helped to launch the record. Soon local radio stations were playing the song and the number one rock and roll outlet, 1050 CHUM, really gave it some good play. Soon it was at the top of the chart knocking out Petula Clark's "My

Love" from the top spot. Nancy Sinatra's "These Boots Are Made for Walking" toppled the Shack tune two weeks later, but the song stayed popular with Maple Leaf fans for a long time.

Eddie Shack carries off the 1963 Stanley Cup after he scored the Cup winning goal on April 18, 1963. (York University Archives/*Toronto Telegram* Collection)

A sample of some of the lyrics includes:

"…So, clear the track, here come Shack. He knocks them down and gives them a whack. He can score goals, he's got a knack, Eddie, Eddie, Shack…"

These words did not win the song a Grammy Award but it did describe the man known as the "Entertainer" pretty accurately! Shack would score 239 career goals and 465 points in 1,047 NHL games with six different teams to go along with four Stanley Cups—all earned as a Maple Leaf.

47 Five Best Maple Leaf Songs

1. **"Clear the Track, Here Comes Shack"**—Top-of-the-charts hit based on the play of winger Eddie Shack.
2. **"Honky the Christmas Goose"**—Leaf goalie Johnny Bower sang about a goose who thought he was no use.
3. **"Leafs Are the Best/The Playoffs Are Here"**—Put together by Leaf winger Glenn Anderson and highlights the musical talents of the 1992–93 Maple Leafs.
4. **"Fifty Mission Cap"**—A song about Leaf legend Bill Barilko by Canadian rock group The Tragically Hip.
5. **"Free to Be"**—An anthem for Leafs nation put together by Alan Frew of musical group Glass Tiger, featuring the refrain "Go Leafs Go."

Best of them all might be "The Maple Leaf Forever," A video tribute by Tim Thompson to an amazing song by Ron Hawkins & The Do-Good Assassins called "Peace & Quiet."

48 Billy Harris

You might think that a well-known hockey writer would come up with the book that should be considered the best volume about Maple Leaf team history. While there are many Leaf history books written by many of the best hockey writers in the business, the top one comes from the pen and camera of a former Toronto player—one of the most popular in team history.

Billy Harris was born in Toronto in 1935 and as a youngster he recalled how he listened to the radio when the Maple Leafs won the Stanley Cup in 1942. He grew up playing minor and junior hockey in the Maple Leaf chain of teams. A highly skilled centre, Harris got his first taste of winning when he was with the Memorial Cup champion Marlboros in 1955. He graduated to the Leafs for the 1955–56 season and was a Maple Leaf for the next decade which included three championships. A very good playmaker, Harris recorded 20 or more assists five times. Harris was also a very reliable two-way centre and had his best season when he scored 22 goals and 30 assists in 1958–59, a year that saw the Leafs get back to the playoffs and make it all the way to the Stanley Cup final.

During the first half of the 1960s, Harris would take his own photos in the dressing room and around the rink. His photos formed the basis of the book entitled, *The Glory Years: Memories of a Decade 1955–65* which also featured Harris' recollections of the time that saw the Leafs regain glory and win three consecutive Stanley Cups. The book also features many great action shots of the era along with some posed photos to give this book a unique and varied combination of photography. Harris' photos are very personal and capture a happy time in Leafs history.

As the team got better with Red Kelly, Dave Keon and Bob Pulford taking over the three main centre spots, Harris became content to be more of a backup, but he certainly contributed when called upon by Leafs coach Punch Imlach. After the Leafs were ousted in the 1965 playoffs to Montreal, Harris was traded to Detroit in a multi-player deal with Toronto receiving defenseman Marcel Pronovost and forward Larry Jeffrey in return—two players who helped the Leafs win the Cup once again in 1967. Harris may have been dealt away but in the hearts of many he was always a Maple Leaf. Harris returned to Maple Leaf Gardens in the 1970s when he coached the Toronto Toros of the WHA for two seasons.

Harris' book which was published in 1989 is a must read for any Maple Leaf fan with the photography holding the readers' interest as much as the text does.

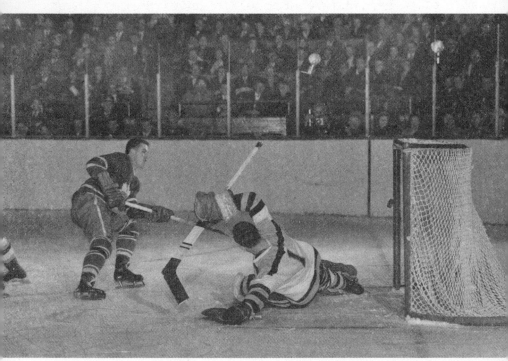

Billy Harris scores against Boston goalie Terry Sawchuk. (Harold Barkley Archives)

49 Best Maple Leafs Team History Books

1. *The Toronto Maple Leaf Hockey Club: Official Centennial Publication* by Kevin Shea and Jason Wilson.

2. *The Glory Years* by Billy Harris—Written by a revered Maple Leaf player covering the decade 1955 to 1965.

3. *The Leafs I Knew* by Scott Young—Well-known hockey writer describes how the Leafs rose to prominence starting in 1958.

4. *Hockey Dynasty* by Jack Batten—One of the first books covering the entire history of the team.

5. *The Top 100 Maple Leafs of All Time* by Mike Leonetti and John Iaboni—Ranking of the greatest players in team history from 1 to 100.

6. *The Maple Leafs: The First 50 Years* by Stan Obodiac—A look at Leaf history after 50 years of existence, filled with great photos in a coffee-table format.

7. *Toronto Maple Leafs: Diary of a Dynasty, 1957–1967* by Kevin Shea and Paul Patskou—Complete account of the decade of Leafs' greatest years.

8. *Hockey, Heartaches, and Hal* by Gord Stellick—One-year general manager describes working for the Leafs in 1970s and 1980s.

9. *The Leafs in Autumn* by Jack Batten—A look at the dominating Maple Leafs of the 1940s.

10. *Hockey Night in Canada* by Foster Hewitt—Legendary broadcaster tells the story of his most memorable days in early hockey broadcasting.

50 Andy Bathgate and Dave Andreychuk

Collecting hockey cards is one of the true joys of being a fan of the game. Hockey cards featuring photos of current players on the front have existed for years.. They were produced on a consistent basis starting in the early 1950s and have been mass marketed on a yearly basis. Some of the sets issued in the 1950s and 1960s are quite beautiful and simply displayed on cardboard. Each year featured different backgrounds to distinguish them from previous seasons— even though player photos were sometimes the same. Youngsters everywhere bought and traded cards while trying to secure the entire set and the hobby proved to be a great pastime—well before cards became highly sought after "collectibles" sometime in the late 1980s.

One of the best issues ever put out was the 1964–65 "Tallboys" set produced by the Topps company out of New York (even though the cards were printed in Canada). These cards were called "Tallboys" because they were longer (21/2" by 411/16") than the cards previously issued and therefore horizontal in appearance. The extra length made the cards stand out more and gave the buyer a much bigger picture of the player than ever before and on a colourful background. The team nickname appeared at the top of each card for all six teams while the back featured the 1963–64 record of the player pictured on the front. A very small biographical note (in both English and French) was also included as well as a cartoon with another small anecdote about the player.

The Maple Leaf players in this card set include the members of the 1964 Stanley Cup, including Andy Bathgate and Don McKenney, the two players Toronto picked up in a deal with the New York Rangers in February of '64. Both players contributed strongly to the Leafs '64 championship run, but it was Bathgate who scored two game-winning goals in the final versus Detroit—including the Stanley Cup winning goal in the seventh game of the series played at Maple Leaf Gardens on April 25, 1964. Bathgate stole the puck at the Leaf blueline and then sped in alone before putting a shot over the shoulder of Detroit goalie Terry Sawchuk for a 1–0 lead. The Leafs would win the game 4–0 and Bathgate

Dave Andreychuk (#14) came to Toronto in a trade with Buffalo. (Dennis Miles)

was pleased he was able to fulfill the expectations of why Toronto had acquired him in a seven-player deal (he finished with nine points in 14 playoff games). It was the only Stanley Cup for the Hall of Fame right winger.

The front of Bathgate's "Tallboy" Maple Leafs card shows a head and shoulder close up of the former New York Rangers captain while the back note on card number 86 indicates that he was traded to the Maple Leafs and that he held the Rangers' all-time scoring mark. It also noted that he had scored 275 career goals and that his 40 goals in 1958–59 was his career best. The cartoon caption indicated he was the winner of the Hart Trophy (most valuable player) in '58–'59. In 1963–64 Bathgate scored 19 goals

Andy Bathgate scored the Stanley Cup winning goal in 1964. (York University Archives/*Toronto Telegram* Collection)

and added a league leading 58 assists for 71 points while playing with New York and Toronto. Prices for this card will vary widely based on condition (as it will for the complete set), but there is no doubt Bathgate's card is one of the most valued (out of 110 total cards) since he is a Hall of Fame player. Thirty years later in 1994, the Fleer card company issued a new set of "Tallboys" for the 1993–94 season. These cards featured an action shot of the player in front plus a second, smaller action shot on the back along with yearly statistics. Unlike the '64–'65 issue, these cards are very glossy and on much stronger paper. The cards are not called "Tallboys" even though they look very retro, but the term "Power Play" is on the front of each card and the set consists of 520 cards.

One of the best cards in the set is Dave Andreychuk of the Maple Leafs. The big right winger was acquired in a deal with Buffalo in February of 1993 and he would finish the '92–'93 season with 54 goals (25 were scored as a Maple Leaf) and 99 points. In the '93 playoffs Andreychuk scored a club-record 12 postseason goals, but unlike Bathgate he fell short of the Stanley Cup since the Leafs were eliminated in the Western Conference final. Many of the Leafs who took Toronto to within one game of the '93 final are featured in the slickly produced and sharp looking set, but they have nowhere near the value of the "Original Six Tallboy" set which would cost thousands of dollars in mint condition. However, either set featuring some of the best Maple Leaf players of all time would be worthy to collect.

Andreychuk played in 223 regular season games as a Maple Leaf and recorded 219 points, including 120 goals. Bathgate played in a total 70 games with Toronto and recorded 63 points.

51 Autry Erickson and Milan Marcetta

The Maple Leafs roster that won the Stanley Cup in 1967 is filled with familiar names. Names engraved on the silver trophy include Armstrong Bower, Horton, Stanley, Keon, Mahovlich, Pulford, Sawchuk and Baun to name a few. All those players were multiple winners of hockey's greatest trophy but look more closely at the roster listing and you will see two names that really stand out because their inclusion is so odd.

Defenseman Autry Erickson (one game) and forward Milan Marcetta (three games) only played in the '67 postseason for the Maple Leafs during their respective careers yet each has their name on the Cup with all the more recognizable Toronto stars. How did this happen? During the era of the "Original Six" teams were allowed to dress extra players in the playoffs. Many of the additions saw the game from the bench but some also got into action depending on the circumstances. Erickson and Marcetta were both called up from the Victoria Maple Leafs of the WHL for the NHL playoffs since their club was not seeing any postseason action in their league.

Marcetta had enjoyed a good regular season for the Victoria team with 40 goals and 75 points while Erickson, who had some NHL experience with Boston and Chicago, added 36 points from the blueline. Both players were capable performers but the Leafs had other viable players with more NHL history, including Eddie Joyal, Dick Gamble, Gerry Ehman, Kent Douglas, and Al Arbour, all players for their main farm team, the Rochester Americans. But the hands of Toronto management may have been tied by the sale agreement completed in the summer of 1966 which might have seen the new Americans' ownership restricting who might be called up to Toronto so that the chances of the Americans to win a third consecutive AHL championship (they had won in 1965 and 1966) remained strong and by NHL call-up rules for the playoffs. Or perhaps the Leafs were trying to build up the value of the Victoria club (which was sold in the summer of 1967) by showing they had good players as well.

Neither Erickson or Marcetta recorded a point in the games they appeared in and between them only a two-minute minor penalty (to Erickson) was the only mark on the official record. Yet because both appeared during the final series versus Montreal, their names are on the Cup. It is interesting to note that others more deserving have their names omitted because they appeared in regular season games only.

Forward John Brenneman suited up 41 times (recording 10 points) for the Leafs in '66–'67 while defenseman Kent Douglas dressed for 39 games (recording 14 points before being sent down to Rochester) and are not on the Leafs championship roster. Brenneman played in the NHL with Chicago and New York and his 41 appearances as a Maple Leaf were the most games, he played in one regular season over his 152-game career. Douglas helped the Leafs to the Stanley Cup in 1963 and was named the NHL's rookie of the year that same year. Douglas was also dressed for 43 games in 1963–64 which saw the Leafs win the Cup but once again he is not listed on the championship roster.

Both these players deserve to have their names on the Cup for the '67 championship especially since both played in more than half of the regular season schedule that year which consisted of 70 games. However, the rules at the time stated that a player must appear in at least one playoff game to get his name on the Cup. While it appears to be unfair that two players like Erickson and Marcetta who contributed so little get such a great reward, those were the governing regulations at the time.

In fact, the NHL changed the rules in 1977 to allow a player who had appeared in 40 regular season games and/or made one appearance in the final to get on the Cup roster. In 1994 the league started to consider exceptions to the rule and that is how former Leaf player Eddie Olczyk got this name on the trophy with the '94 New York Rangers even though he did not meet the minimum criteria. Perhaps the same consideration should be given to Brenneman and Douglas who deserve the recognition.

52 Terry Sawchuk

In 2009 the NHL released a collector's edition DVD set featuring 10 great games in the history of the Toronto Maple Leafs. While all the games shown are interesting and capture special moments, there is one that is extraordinary and stands out above the rest.

May 2, 1967, is a date that every Toronto fan who was around at the time will never forget. Not only was it the last game of the 1967 Stanley Cup final between the Maple Leafs and their long-time rival the Montreal Canadiens, it was also the final night of the "Original Six." The NHL was expanding to 12 teams for the 1967–68 campaign so it seemed only fitting that the two oldest members of the league would have one last battle of the soon-to-be extinct six-team era. The game was played at Maple Leafs Gardens and it was a tight contest right down to the last minute of play. The Maple Leafs needed this game desperately since they did not want to return to the Montreal Forum for a seventh game. Their fans could sense the team needed strong support on this night and the chant "Go Leafs Go" could be heard resonating throughout the Gardens all night long.

Anyone watching this game will quickly come to the conclusion that Toronto netminder Terry Sawchuk was the reason the Leafs won this game 3–1 and secured the Stanley Cup for the 11th time. After a scoreless first period, the Leafs opened the scoring on a goal by right winger Ron Ellis. Another tally late in the second by Jim Pappin gave the Leafs a 2–0 lead going into the third. The Leafs enjoyed the lead because Sawchuk was working his magic turning

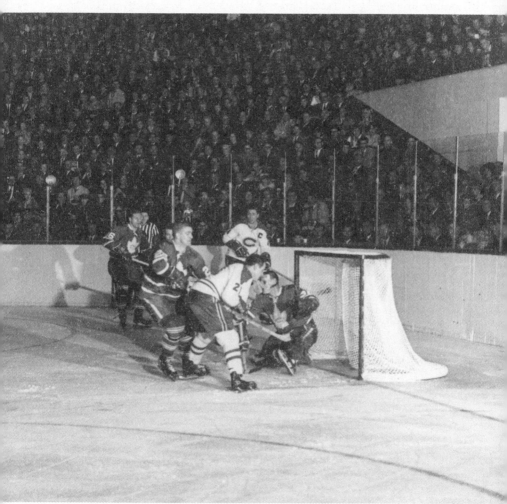

Goalie Terry Sawchuk (#24) stops the Montreal Canadiens in close.
(York University Archives/*Toronto Telegram* Collection)

away one great chance after another. The 37-year-old goalie knew he needed to be great for the Leafs to turn back the speedy Habs and he was equal to the task for two periods.

Early in the third former Leaf winger Dick Duff scored on a beautiful individual effort to make it 2–1 and the tension in the Gardens could be felt for the rest of the contest. Duff's effort was the only drive that eluded Sawchuk as he stopped 40 of 41 shots but the Leafs could only breathe easier when captain George Armstrong put a drive into the empty Montreal net with 47 seconds to play.

"This has to be the greatest thrill of my life," Sawchuk said after the game. "I've had a lot of wonderful moments in hockey and other Stanley Cups (with Detroit) but nothing equals this." Sawchuk also recounted how he had nearly left the team earlier in the season due to a back problem and how he never imagined this ending. Even in the series versus Montreal, Sawchuk had been shelled twice for six goals and many had written him and the Leafs off. However, Sawchuk did not like to be ridiculed and when goaltending partner Johnny Bower was no longer able to play, Sawchuk stepped in and played brilliantly over the last two contests and gave up just two goals. It was the perfect ending to a great career by Sawchuk who was one of the greatest goalies (with 103 career shutouts) of all time.

Sawchuk's performance alone makes this game worth watching for any hockey fan but to see Toronto and Montreal battle for the Stanley Cup is a great slice of Canadiana and that should give this video a special place on the DVD shelf.

53 Best Maple Leafs Videos

1. *The Passion Returns* (1993)—Highlights from the 1992–93 season, featuring Doug Gilmour, Wendel Clark, and more.
2. *75th Forever* (2002)—Toronto Maple Leafs 75th anniversary is celebrated with a complete history of the team.
3. *Forever Rivals* (1996)—A closer look at the Leafs–Canadiens rivalry over the history of both franchises.
4. *Face-Off* (original in 1971, re-issued in 2011)—Movie featuring a young Maple Leaf star and his romance with a singer in the early 1970s. Re-issue includes Second City (SCTV) spoof on the movie.
5. *1967 Stanley Cup*—Home movie taken from rink side of Leafs last Cup, shot by long-time season ticket holder Jim Costick. Set to music and in colour too!

Oldies but Goodies:

1933 Hockey Champions—Foster Hewitt calls final game between Leafs and Rangers with between period interviews.
1945 Puck Chasers—Game footage from Leafs and Detroit in playoffs
1948 Hockey Cavalcade—Colour film of Leafs and Canadiens
1956 Here & There: The Canadian Game—Covers all hockey in Toronto.

54 A Final Face-Off: Allan Stanley

Much has always been made of the face-off in the Toronto end of the rink against Montreal that helped close out the sixth game of the 1967 final. The Leafs were holding on to a slim 2–1 lead with 55 seconds to play but the Canadiens had one last shot with their goalie (Gump Worsley) on the bench and six attackers all in the Leafs zone at Maple Leaf Gardens. As was his custom back then, Toronto coach Punch Imlach sent defenseman Allan Stanley out to take the draw against Montreal centre Jean Beliveau. The other Leafs out on the ice were Red Kelly, Bob Pulford, George Armstrong, and Tim Horton—all in front of goalie Terry Sawchuk. Stanley, who had been taking face-offs all game long, as had all the other Leafs defensemen, occupied Beliveau enough so that the puck was free for Kelly to scoop up and pass to Pulford who hit Armstrong with another relay. The Leafs captain hit the open net after he crossed centre ice and iced the Leafs fourth championship of the 1960s.

When the game was over many felt Imlach's choice of defenders was a sentimental ploy to reward his old guard players and to acknowledge that their time was coming to an end. Imlach may indeed have been motivated by sending his most trusted veterans out in a blaze of glory, but it is interesting to note that he pulled the same trick seven years earlier in a 1960 playoff game versus Detroit!

On March 26, 1960 the Leafs were home to the Red Wings in the second game of the semi-finals. The Leafs needed a win on home ice to even the series at one game each. Toronto had a 3–2 lead but Detroit pulled goalie (ironically enough) Terry Sawchuk for the extra attacker with a face-off in the Leafs end and just 1:08 to play. Out for the Leafs were Stanley, Horton, Pulford, Kelly and

Armstrong—the same exact five skaters as in '67—to defend in front of goalie Johnny Bower. This time Kelly took the face-off but lost it to Gordie Howe.

As the puck was shot behind the Leafs' net, Horton, Stanley and Bower did not let Detroit get the puck out in front before Armstrong snared the loose puck. He quickly passed it to Pulford who cleared the Leaf zone. Detroit regained possession but a pass directed to Norm Ullman was picked off by Pulford who let a shot

Maple Leaf defenseman Allan Stanley (#26) battles against the Montreal Canadiens. (Harold Barkley Archives)

go from his own side of centre and right into the empty Detroit net for an unassisted tally. Same defenders as in '67 and the same result—a Maple Leafs empty net marker to clinch an important game (the Leafs would oust Detroit in six games).

After the Detroit game Imlach was asked about Pulford shooting before reaching the centre red line. "They've got their orders when there's an empty net," the Leafs coach replied. "They've been told a thousand times: get it over the blue line and the red line; we've got the goal: don't need another one; just keep them from getting one; I told Pulford when he came to the bench." Spoken like a true hockey coach, but the most important thing was the Leafs held on and Imlach had to be happy about that in both 1960 and 1967. Same strategy, same players and same result and it should be mentioned there was no shot on the Leafs net taken by either Detroit or Montreal. Both Leaf goals were scored at 19:13 of the third period.

One of the most important defenders in either case was Stanley, a slow moving but very effective blueliner who the Leafs had acquired in a 1958 trade with Boston—one of the best deals in team history. Stanley would help anchor four Stanley Cup championships and in the final minute of the '67 final it was burly number 26 who re-positioned Kelly to allow him to get at the puck a split second before Montreal's Yvan Cournoyer would have reached the loose disk.

Allan Stanley died in October of 2013 at the age of 87. He was a very deserving member of the Hockey Hall of Fame.

55 The Mysterious Trophy

It was in 1964 that the Board of Directors at Maple Leaf Gardens decided they would honour former Maple Leafs owner and manager Conn Smythe with a trophy bearing his name. The award, which was also approved by the NHL Board of Governors, was to be given out each year (starting in 1965) to recognize the top performer during the NHL playoffs. The trophy had a replica of Maple Leaf Gardens sitting on a base with a Maple Leaf rising above the building. Smythe very much appreciated the honour and it is still one of the most prestigious awards in all of hockey. Jean Beliveau of Montreal was the first winner of the Smythe Trophy followed by Roger Crozier of Detroit in 1966.

When the Maple Leafs won the Stanley cup in 1967 there were a few candidates to consider for the Smythe Trophy. Jim Pappin led all postseason scorers with 15 points while line mate Peter Stemkowski had 12 points and played very aggressively throughout the playoffs. Goaltenders Terry Sawchuk and to a lesser extent Johnny Bower also deserved mention. However, for many there was really only one man to consider and that was the tireless Dave Keon. The stylish centre had done it all for Toronto—back check, fore-check, winning face-offs, scoring goals and playing superb defense. Emile Francis, the coach and general manager of the New York Rangers, said that the Leafs could win with either Sawchuk or Bower but they couldn't win the Cup without Keon. "He is one of the finest centres in the NHL because he can do so many things for you," Francis said. "On many occasions throughout the play-offs you see this guy killing penalties, taking his regular turn, and winning those big face-offs."

The Smythe Trophy was presented two days after the Stanley Cup was awarded (the only time this ever happened) because the league's Board of Governors believed that two presentations in one evening were too much. The Smythe Trophy was formally announced at the Hot Stove Lounge of Maple Leaf Gardens by Don Ruck, the newly-named publicity director for the NHL. Six league governors or representatives cast ballots for the MVP after the Stanley Cup championship contest. NHL president Clarence Campbell took the sealed envelopes to Montreal, where they were counted. One ballot indicated Terry Sawchuk as the most valuable playoff performer, but five selected Dave Keon, to receive the coveted Conn Smythe Trophy.

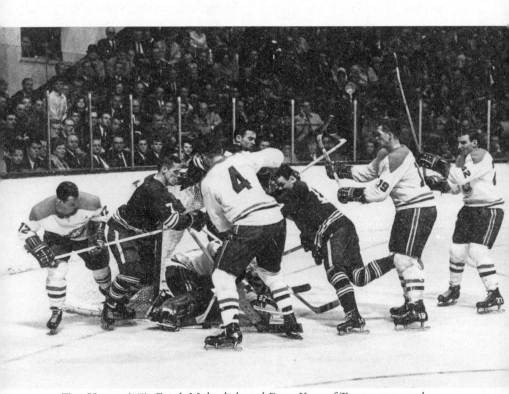

Tim Horton (#7), Frank Mahovlich and Dave Keon of Toronto swarm the Montreal net during the 1967 Stanley Cup final. (York University Archives/ *Toronto Telegram* Collection)

But there was an additional presentation that day. Surprisingly, Sawchuk was awarded the Air Canada Trophy as the Leafs' most valuable playoff performer, and with it a flight for two anywhere the airline flew. Why an MVP trophy was presented to Sawchuk while the Conn Smythe Trophy was awarded to Keon is indeed a mystery, but the even bigger question is, whatever became of this award? The Hockey Hall of Fame has no record of it. The Sawchuk family is aware that the goalie won the award and believes that the Leaf players themselves voted on who should receive the award. Originally, this trophy was engraved as Trans-Canada Airlines, which meant it was at least commissioned prior to 1965 when the carrier changed its name to Air Canada.

Maple Leaf Sports and Entertainment has never heard of it and Air Canada could find nothing in their files. The Air Canada Trophy apparently was never awarded again. But at least Sawchuk did get some well-deserved recognition for his stellar play (winning a total of six of the eight games needed to capture the championship)—even though not many people were aware of it then or now. However, there are photos of Sawchuk with the trophy, and the inscription on the award indicates it was given to a Maple Leaf player for "outstanding team work."

56 The 1967–68 Season

Even though "the Great Expansion" of 1967 hurt the Maple Leafs (all the "Original Six" teams lost players to the six new NHL clubs), the Toronto side still had a good nucleus of top talent to start the 1967–68 campaign. In fact, after 35 games that season, Toronto had only allowed 78 goals against while posting a respectable

17–12–6 mark—good for third place in what was now known as the East Division of the NHL. Their 40-point total had them only five points behind second place Chicago with two games in hand. However, the second half of the year exposed the Leafs weaknesses and they gradually tumbled out of a playoff spot.

In his book, *Hockey is a Battle*, Toronto coach and general manager Punch Imlach saw a problem with his team the night of November 5, 1967, when they rolled into Boston for a Sunday night game. The game ended in a 2–2 tie but during that contest Leaf winger Brian Conacher accidently cut Bobby Orr with his stick and that led to a bench-clearing brawl. Orr went ballistic on the much more mild-mannered Conacher who was concerned about getting punched in the face while wearing contact lenses. The Leafs player covered up as best he could, but it took too long for his teammates to respond to the Boston charge.

If players like Bob Baun (lost to Oakland) and Eddie Shack (traded to Boston) had still been with the Leafs, it might have been a different story. Some of the Leaf veterans, such as George Armstrong and Bob Pulford, were too old to be considered a physical threat anymore while Boston had younger guys eager to become the "Big Bad Bruins." And Conacher was not quite the same after his battle with Orr and his performance in the 1967 playoffs (featuring timely goals, some toughness plus effective penalty-killing duties) soon became a fond memory.

Lack of toughness was just one problem that the Leafs could not overcome. Imlach would not reunite the best line in the previous playoffs separating Bob Pulford from Pete Stemkowski and Jim Pappin. In short order all three of these players were gone despite their significant contribution to the '67 championship. Dealing Pappin to Chicago for a fading Pierre Pilote was especially difficult for any Leaf fan to watch. The goaltending issue was never addressed with aging Johnny Bower and journeyman Bruce Gamble minding the Leaf net. They gave the Leafs their best but it was obvious Toronto needed some new blood in goal. The defensemen were very experienced, but far too slow for a much faster league starting in '67–'68. Centre Dave Keon was never right that year because of a leg injury, and scored only 11 goals—a totally unexpected performance from one of the best players in the NHL.

The Leafs might have made it to the postseason if they had a better record against the six new teams, but they were a paltry 8–13–3 in 24 games against the expansion clubs and that sealed their fate. They finished the year 33–31–10, good enough for 76 points but in fifth place in the East, four points out of the playoffs. All of the teams in the West Division were sharp and ready to play the defending champs while the Leafs were simply not ready for that challenge. The one bright spot for the Leafs was the performance of Mike Walton who scored a team-best 30 goals and 59 points despite never seeing eye-to-eye with Imlach.

The Leafs' disappointing performance as the '67–'68 season moved along led to the trading of legendary winger Frank Mahovlich to Detroit in March of 1968. It was a franchise changing deal that brought about a good return but not nearly as much as the Leafs gave up. The trade made the Leafs a skilled but very small team up front while two youngsters like Stemkowski and Garry Unger were now wearing a red and white sweater. The trade gave the Leafs some new life, but it was too late to make the '68 postseason ensuring the Leafs had gone from champions to out of the playoffs in one year. Some might argue the franchise never recovered from the year the team died in '67–'68.

57 Jean-Paul Parise

A Wednesday night game at Maple Leaf Gardens on November 15, 1967 between the Maple Leafs and the Boston Bruins had a number of interesting storylines present. The Leafs were the reigning Stanley Cup champions but the NHL's "Great Expansion" had taken away much of their valued experience from their championship roster. As a result, the Toronto side had lost much of their swagger. The revamped Boston Bruins were vastly improved with a new strategy combining talent and intimidation. A young phenom name Bobby Orr was just starting to dominate while an off-season trade landed them a big centre in Phil Esposito. And, since it was Boston's first visit to Toronto that season, it was Eddie Shack's return to his old arena where he was known as "The Entertainer" and was loved by Leaf fans and soon he would be loathed by them. It was also Leaf defenseman Tim Horton's 999th career game. Only three players in NHL history up to that point had played 1,000 NHL games with the same team—Gordie Howe and Alex Delvecchio with Detroit and Harry Howell with New York.

Dave Keon, the Leafs best centre, was out with a charley horse—a medical term common in the day but virtually nonexistent now—and the Leafs' best player, Frank Mahovlich, was also out as he was hospitalized with depression and tension issues (it was widely speculated that this was induced by coach Punch Imlach). As a result, Mike Walton centred the Leafs top line with captain George Armstrong and a left winger named Jean-Paul Parise who was going to play his first game for Toronto in place of the Big M. Parise was called up from the Rochester Americans of the AHL and would wear sweater number 17.

Walton turned out to be the star of the game with a hat trick, but Parise left his mark as well. On one of Walton's first period tallies, the hardworking Parise did most of the leg work by fighting off no less than Orr's checking efforts for the puck and deftly sliding the disk to the face-off circle to a waiting Walton who backhanded the puck past a surprised Gerry Cheevers in the Boston net. Not only did Parise demonstrate an offensive flair, he also proved he was sound defensively. At the end of the 4–2 victory for Toronto, the Smooth Rock Falls, Ontario native skated out as the third star of the game as selected by the legendary broadcaster Foster Hewitt to cap off a memorable debut as a Maple Leaf!

With all the storylines surrounding the game, Parise's debut created a new interest and Leaf fans were looking forward to cheering on the 26-year-old winger for many years to come. However, the Leafs had to return Parise back to Rochester since he had only been "loaned" to them for just this one game. The Leafs did not own Parise's contract because he was the property of the independently owned Americans. After Parise's sterling effort against Boston, Joe Crozier, the Rochester coach and G.M., asked Imlach to send him back immediately. The Americans had dealt for Parise in October of 1967 in a trade involving Gerry Ehman, a player that the Leafs were forced to provide the Rochester club by their new owners when they purchased the team from the Maple Leafs. Crozier then astutely traded the 35-year-old Ehman, a once valued member of the Leafs in the late 50s and early 60s, to the Oakland Seals for Parise and Bryan Hextall, Jr. Parise had been selected by the Seals in the expansion draft from the Bruins organization (where he had played in 21 NHL games for Boston) after playing very well in minor league cities like Kingston, Minneapolis and Oklahoma City.

The potential shown by Parise was noticed not only by Imlach but also by other teams in the expanded NHL including the Minnesota North Stars. In need of more players, Crozier started accepting offers for Parise and deemed Imlach's proposal inadequate since the Leafs minor league reserves had been reduced considerably when they sold off the Americans and the Victoria Maple Leafs of the Western Hockey League just as the NHL was expanding. Parise was traded to the North Stars along with Milan Marcetta for five players and the loan of a badly needed goaltender. Toronto had lost out on a good player who could have helped the team out in the transition from the "Original Six" to the expansion era.

Parise became a star with the Minnesota North Stars playing in two NHL All-Star Games with a career high of 75-points during 1972–73, after participating in the famous 1972 Summit Series for Team Canada against the Soviets. He was a valuable two-way player throughout his NHL career and would score 238 goals. He played in 890 career games but only one for the Maple Leafs!

Zach Parise, J.P.'s son, is a current NHL star with the Minnesota Wild.

58 Tim Horton

On March 3, 1970, while the Maple Leafs were on the American West Coast to play the California Seals, they traded the heart and soul of the team away to the New York Rangers. Defenseman Tim Horton who anchored the Leafs blueline for four Stanley Cups and six trips to the final was dealt away to the New York club, who was desperate for defensive help with a couple of regulars out of their lineup and the playoffs looming. The Leafs were able to shed an $85,000 a year salary (Toronto owner Harold Ballard said the team would not pay that much for Horton when they were going to miss the playoffs in any event) with the Rangers promising to deliver "four or five players" according to Ballard once the season was over. The 40-year-old Horton agreed to the deal but the Leafs did not provide any names of the players that would be coming to Toronto later on.

"It comes as a bit of a jolt, to think about leaving the Leafs," Horton said once the deal was done. "But I understand their position completely. They have to think of the future now. And if they can get some younger fellows in exchange for an older guy like me, they're wise to do it. It's the sensible thing to do really," Horton

The Maple Leafs were never the same after they traded away defenseman Tim Horton. (Harold Barkley Archives)

concluded, even though he cried when told the news. Horton had been kept informed all along but it was still a shock when it was made official.

The Leafs were not sure if Horton was coming back for the 1970–71 season as retirement talk was always around the defenseman. Horton was one of the owners of a still young but thriving coffee and donut business and was unsure if hockey could be squeezed into his demanding schedule. Horton first brought the business to light during a *Hockey Night in Canada* interview with Ward Cornell on October 26, 1968, during the Leafs 2–0 win over the Boston Bruins on a Saturday night. "Things are quite hectic trying to combine hockey and business," Horton stated. Cornell inquired if he was talking about his new donut chain. "Yes," replied Horton, "Tim Horton Donuts…It's nice of you to let me get a word in about it." Cornell wanted to change the subject (likely because the bosses at HNIC and CBC would not like giving away free advertising), but Horton persisted and thanked people from Hamilton and Burlington for helping to launch his new venture. Horton thanked other cities while Cornell slipped a bill as a charge for the promotion. It might not have been the smoothest start to a new venture but Horton was determined to be successful after he had failed at other businesses bearing his name (hamburger places and car lots).

The Rangers lost out in the 1970 playoffs to the Boston Bruins, but Horton came back to Broadway for the '70–'71 campaign and helped to eliminate the Leafs in a six-game quarter-final series. As for the players received by the Leafs, included were two career minor league players (Guy Trottier and Denis Dupere). Those two were useful players for the Leafs in '70–'71 but the main return was veteran goalie Jacques Plante who was named to the NHL's second all-star team in 1971. All things considered, it was not much of a return for the best Maple Leaf defenseman in team history who had played in 1,185 career games for Toronto and was a six-time league all-star. Plante was later moved to Boston in 1973 getting the Leafs a first-round draft choice back that they used to select Ian Turnbull, giving Toronto something tangible from the Horton deal even if it was four years later.

Horton passed away at the age of 44 after a car accident just as his business was starting to gather momentum and sell more franchises. The marketing power of the Maple Leafs proved itself once again as the coffee and donut enterprise grew with the name of one of the greatest players in team history. It is unlikely that the business would have flourished had it not been for Horton being a Toronto Maple Leaf. Tim Hortons' (the stores still bear his name) is one of the greatest ventures in Canadian business history, still going strong years later.

59 Ernie Moser in 1969

When the NHL implemented the first ever "amateur draft" in 1963, its purpose was to phase out the sponsorship of junior hockey teams by the six NHL teams at the time. The "Original Six" teams had been able to recruit and sign players as early as fourteen and assign them to junior teams in their system by having them sign the infamous "C" Form that bound the player for life to that particular organization. Toronto Maple Leaf president Stafford Smythe was the driving force behind the implementation of the amateur draft system despite knowing the longtime advantages that the two Canadian teams had previously would be gone. If expansion were to happen (as it did in 1967), the NHL had to be ready to do away with sponsorship and use a draft system to divide up the incoming talent.

Since most of the graduating junior players were already tied to their NHL teams via the "C" Form, it took until 1969 before the amateur draft would be truly functional as any sponsored player under the old system would have graduated by then. However, it wasn't completely free and clear to draft any junior player who had finished their junior eligibility. The Montreal Canadiens still had the option of using their "cultural" benefit by selecting the best two French-Canadian players prior to the actual draft. Using this unique rule for the final time, the Habs selected star juniors Rejean Houle and Marc Tardif. Fortunately for the rest of the league, the NHL board of governors declined to continue this special cultural by-law commencing in the 1970 amateur draft. Imagine if Montreal had been able to select native Quebecers like Gilbert Perreault and Dale Tallon in 1970 and Guy Lafleur and Marcel Dionne in 1971. Otherwise, the new universal draft system meant that NHL teams would get a chance at the best juniors available in reverse order of finish.

Drafting of players not officially signed by NHL teams had been taking place since 1963 (usually a three- or four-round process) and the Leafs had done a fairly good job of selecting by taking the likes of Walt McKechnie, Jim McKenny, Mike Pelyk, Jim Dorey, Rick Ley, and Brad Selwood. They mysteriously missed out on Brad Park, a star with the Toronto Marlies, and Peter Mahovlich (whom they wanted to play with his brother Frank in a Maple Leaf uniform), but they had selected nine players between 1963 and 1968 that would play in the NHL.

In 1969 the Leafs were selecting ninth overall and were hoping the scouting staff led by former Leaf player, captain and longtime chief scout Bob Davidson could continue to unearth top prospects in the expanded draft (now 10 rounds in length and all 12 NHL teams selecting) as he did previously by recruiting individually, which had resulted in Memorial Cups for the Marlboros in 1955 and 1956 and again in 1964 and 1967, along with the St. Mike's championship in 1961. The bulk of the Leaf Stanley Cup teams in the '60s had been built with juniors from the sponsored Marlboros and St. Mike's teams.

Davidson hired three scouts to cover Western Canada and when it was time for their first selection they went with Ernie Moser, a 6', 178-pound forward from the Estevan Bruins of the WCHL. Moser had respectable numbers in 1968–69 with Estevan, scoring 46 goals and totaling 86 points, and it was thought that Davidson had Moser rated the top prospect in the entire draft. Moser, however, was assigned to the Tulsa Oilers, the Maple Leafs main farm team, for the 1969–70 season and he produced 28 points, including 10 goals, in 55 games. The Leafs soon forgot about Moser who became a career minor league player. The Leafs 1969–70 media guide does not feature any write-up on their first-round draft pick even though Doug Brindley (selected 20th overall in '69 and would play in three career games with the Leafs) gets a small biography in the guide. While two other players the Leafs drafted in '69 (Larry McIntyre and Brian Spencer), also made it to the NHL, the Leafs first major foray (six picks in total) into the larger universal draft was pretty much a disaster.

The worst part of it all was that they passed on the chance to select Bobby Clarke out of Flin Flon, Manitoba when they had the chance. Other teams also passed on Clarke because of his juvenile diabetes but the feisty centre had led the WHL in points for three consecutive seasons and he seemed a perfect fit for the type of player the Leafs could call their own. Years later, Clarke would express disappointment that many teams like the Leafs passed on the opportunity to take him in the '69 draft and expressed the opinion that Moser was not even a top player in the WHL at the time. Moser would primarily play out his eight-year pro career in the old International Hockey League, widely considered an inferior hockey circuit.

Clarke would be selected by the Philadelphia Flyers 17th overall at the strong urging of scout Gerry Melnyk (who did his research on the disease Clarke was battling), and would go on to a Hall of Fame career which would see him win two Stanley Cups as team captain. If the Leafs had chosen Clarke in '69 and followed up with Darryl Sittler (8th overall in 1970), the Toronto club would have had the top two centres in hockey as they did in the glory years of the 1940s and 1960s.

60 Ten Worst First-Round Draft Picks

1. **Ernie Moser in 1969**—Never played a game for the Maple Leafs.
2. **Bob Neely in 1973**—The second of three first-round picks that year. He was never the same dominating player as he was in junior, despite a high skill level.
3. **Jim Benning in 1981**—He was supposed to be an offensively gifted defenseman, but his skating was too much of a detriment.
4. **Scott Pearson in 1988**—This big winger looked like a good choice, but injuries slowed him down and was dealt to Quebec. Leafs passed on Jeremy Roenick.
5. **Steve Bancroft in 1989**—The third of three first-round picks that year played a grand total of six NHL games in his career—none for Leafs.
6. **Drake Berehowsky in 1990**—Talented defenseman hampered by knee problems.

7. **Brandon Convery in 1992**—Smallish right-handed shooting centre played in just 50 games for Leafs before he was traded to Vancouver.
8. **Jeff Ware in 1995**—Leafs picked this defenseman for all the wrong reasons and played just 15 games for Toronto.
9. **Luca Cereda in 1999**—Questionable pick at best and health issues derailed any chance he had to play in the NHL.
10. **Jiri Tlusty in 2006**—He was supposed to be a smooth-skating goal scorer but Leafs dumped him to Carolina for nothing in 2009.

61 Ten Best First-Round Picks Since 1969

1. **Darryl Sittler**—Hall of Fame player chosen 8th overall in 1970. Still remains the Leafs best all-time first-round choice.
2. **Lanny McDonald**—Hall of Fame player chosen 4th overall in 1973. Should never have been traded away.
3. **Wendel Clark**—Chosen first overall by the Leafs in 1985 and had a major impact on the team when healthy.
4. **Austin Matthews**—Chosen first overall in the 2016 draft; may eventually be the best Leaf pick.
5. **Ian Turnbull**—Chosen 15th overall in 1973 and still holds team record for most goals in one season by a defenseman with 22.
6. **Vincent Damphousse**—Chosen sixth overall in 1986 and would go on to record 1,205 career points.
7. **Mitch Marner**—Chosen fourth overall in the 2016 draft despite Leaf coach Babcock preferring a defenseman. Will get better.

Morgan Rielly poses with general manager Dave Nonis (left) and director of amateur scouting Dave Morrison (right) after being chosen fifth overall in the 2012 draft. (AP Images)

8. **Al Iafrate**—Chosen fourth overall in 1984 and had all the tools to be great but too immature during time as a Leaf. Leafs got good return when he was traded to Washington for Peter Zezel and Bob Rouse.

9. **John Anderson**—Chosen 11th overall in 1977 and was a consistent performer before being dealt away in another bad trade. Anderson scored 282 career goals.

10. **Morgan Rielly**—Chosen fifth overall in 2012 with the Leafs hoping they had a superstar in the making. He recorded 27 points (2G, 25A) as a rookie in 2013–14.

62 Four Bench-Clearing Brawls

As the middle of December was passed during the 2013–14 NHL season, a total of 113 games worth of suspensions had been dealt out by the "Player Safety" department of the league office. Fans and many hockey observers called for a ban on all fighting as a way of toning down hostilities on the ice, including hits from behind and "head shots" to unaware or unsuspecting opponents. By the end of the regular season the total number of games that players were suspended for reached 178 (a total that included 16 pre-season games) and another 29 playoff games were handed out as of May 31ˢᵗ—and that was before the Stanley Cup final even began!

Perhaps a little historical perspective on NHL violence might be in order here. During the 1970–71 season the Toronto Maple Leafs engaged in four bench-clearing brawls—three in the regular season and one in the playoffs. It all started on December 9, 1970, when the Leafs shut out the Montreal Canadiens 4–0 on home ice. A major fight broke out with Leaf defenseman Jim Dorey (no stranger to fighting) going at it with Claude Larose (a well-known agitator) of the Habs. Soon everyone on both benches spilled out onto the ice. Rick Ley of the Leafs squared off with Marc Tardif and Mickey Redmond while scrappy Leaf centre Jim Harrison took on Terry Harper of Montreal. For good measure Leafs rookie Darryl Sittler started swinging with Bill Collins of the Canadiens. A total of $14,550 in fines was dished out by the NHL office but that did nothing to deter the Leafs.

Just 18 days later the Toronto club staged another donnybrook on home ice against the Philadelphia Flyers on December 26, 1970, during a 9–1 Leaf victory. This brawl came late in the game and was sparked by Toronto rookie Brian Spencer who had been

Jim Dorey and Brian Spencer.

brought up from the minors to give the Maple Leafs some added muscle. Spencer's hit on Flyers winger Gary Dornhoefer upset the Philadelphia side unleashing Bob Kelly and Ed Van Impe to settle the score. The benches emptied once more but it was a little tamer than the brawl with Montreal earlier in the month.

Less than a month later the Leafs were at it again, this time in Los Angeles against the Kings on January 23, 1971. The Leafs took exception to Eddie Joyal (an ex-Leaf) running over goalie Jacques Plante. This action enraged Toronto hard rock defenseman Bob Baun who chased Joyal down the ice. Dorey also went at it with Paul Curtis of the Kings in another main bout while all the players came off the ice in this first period skirmish. This time the Leafs were beaten 3–2 to end their string of wins when large brawls took place.

The final bench-clearing action of the year took place in New York against the Rangers on April 8, 1971. It was a feisty playoff contest throughout, but the Leafs were clearly in charge leading 4–1 late in the third period when all the fights broke out. Harrison and Baun took turns duking it out with Vic Hadfield and Spencer was the first off the bench when things got out of hand. Sittler and Brad Park left the penalty box to join the melee and started another fight. Leaf goalie Bernie Parent lost his mask when Hadfield flung it into the crowd at Madison Square Garden and could not get it back. Total fines for this nasty brawl was a combined figure of over $14,000.

The Leafs were not the only team (the Canadiens and the Bruins had an ugly situation spill into the stands at the Boston Garden) to engage in these sorts of fights which were quite common place back then—even in the playoffs (although it was generally rare in the postseason). The bench-clearing era of fighting is something of the distant past but no one seemed too upset back then, perhaps because they happened fairly frequently. The air was cleared and the teams returned to playing hockey without any government inquires being held (those were conducted later when brawling became an almost every game occurrence). When the violent nature of the modern NHL is discussed it is clear that a look back shows the game was much harsher in the early 1970s, and then the Flyers began their days as the "Broad Street Bullies," which made it considerably worse for a number of years.

Did all the brawling help the Maple Leafs, who had started the '70–'71 season so poorly? They came on to finish the year with 37 wins and earned a playoff spot with 82 points.

63 Jacques Plante and Bernie Parent

After a legendary career with the Montreal Canadiens (which saw him win a total of six Stanley Cups and the Vezina Trophy seven times), goaltender Jacques Plante decided he had enough of hockey and decided to retire at the age of 36 after playing two years for the New York Rangers. However, he came back to the NHL at the age of 40 when he joined the St. Louis Blues for the 1968–69 and 1969–70 seasons—two years that saw the Blues make it to the Stanley Cup final. The Maple Leafs then acquired the rights to the 42-year-old netminder for the 1970–71 season in the trade that saw Tim Horton go to the New York Rangers.

The only other proven goaltender on the Leaf roster was veteran Bruce Gamble, who had a big part in getting the Leafs back to the playoffs in 1969 but could not be considered a top netminder. Plante came to the Leafs and provided a veteran presence by posting a 24–11–4 record in 40 games played, and earned a second-team all-star berth in the process. Plante could be an ornery character (no goal scored against him was his own fault), but he was especially good on home ice and that helped the Leafs overcome a bad start to make the playoffs in 1971.

Even though the Leafs were happy with Plante's performance, they also realized they needed a younger netminder for the future. Toronto general manager Jim Gregory dangled forward Mike Walton (a very talented player who was not destined to stay with the Leafs after run-ins with coaches and managers), and was able to secure the rights to Bernie Parent in a three-team deal that also involved Philadelphia and Boston. Acquiring Parent, a native of Montreal, was easily Gregory's best move as the Leafs boss and

Toronto now had one of the best tandems in the NHL with the pair of Quebec-born netminders.

Parent went 7–7–3 over 18 appearances to close out the '70–'71 season and the Leafs would take on the New York Rangers in the first round of the playoffs. Toronto coach Johnny MacLellan decided to go with the veteran Plante to open the series on Broadway but he had a terrible night in a 5–4 Leaf loss that should have been a victory. Parent was in for the next two games—both

Hall of Fame netminder Bernie Parent as a Maple Leaf. (Toronto Maple Leafs)

Leaf wins—but then lost the next two to put the Leafs on the brink of elimination. Plante was given the start on home ice for the sixth game and played very well for the most part. However, in overtime he let in a shot by former Leaf winger Bob Nevin (a drive even Plante admitted he should have stopped), to end the Leaf season. Many believe if Parent had played the whole series the Leafs might have been victorious.

The tandem was back for the entire 1971–72 season but the Leafs were unable to improve, although they did make the playoffs again despite dropping from 82 points to 80 in the regular season. Parent loved learning everything he could from his childhood idol and became a better goalie—much like the Leafs had hoped when they made the deal. Parent's then-wife did not take to the city of Toronto and Parent decided to sign with the new rival league—the World Hockey Association—for the 1972–73 season. The Leafs tried every move available to bring Parent back to the fold but they were too late and too cheap when it mattered most. Eventually Parent returned to Philadelphia and starred for two Stanley Cup winning teams as a Flyer. He was also elected to the Hockey Hall of Fame in 1984.

As for Plante, the native of Shawinigan, Quebec, would play professional hockey until he was 46 years old. The Leafs traded him to Boston in 1973 but the Bruins grew to dislike the quirky veteran so much they could not wait to get him out of Beantown. Plante's final pro season was spent with the WHA Edmonton Oilers in 1974–75. He was elected to the Hall of Fame in 1978.

64 Rick Ley, Brad Selwood, and Guy Trottier

When the Maple Leafs ended the 1971–72 season after losing to the Boston Bruins once again in the playoffs, there were a number of players who had to be re-signed or risk losing them to the WHA. Goalie Bernie Parent was the first to go, signing with the Miami team of the new league, but he never played a game for the "Screaming Eagles" having to be moved to the Philadelphia franchise in the new venture. No matter where he went, Parent's loss was disastrous for the Maple Leafs and felt for many years. But there were other players the Leafs general manager was unable to get signed to a new contract.

Centre Jim Harrison was prominent since he had given the Leafs a grinding third line centre (86 points) with a feisty presence (248 penalty minutes) in 175 career games in Toronto. He was definitely behind Dave Keon and Norm Ullman, but he was tough to play against. He left for the Edmonton team in the WHA and recorded a 10-point night for the squad known as the Alberta Oilers for the 1972–73 season. Harrison's departure opened up a centre ice spot for Darryl Sittler although that was eventually going to happen in any event.

The next significant players to go were defenseman Rick Ley and Brad Selwood—two youngsters who looked like they had a good future ahead of them. Ley played so well for the New England Whalers (later known as the Hartford Whalers), they eventually retired his sweater number two while Selwood gave the Whalers seven strong seasons. Jim Dorey was traded away by the Leafs in 1972 to the New York Rangers (for Pierre Jarry) but he also ended up with the Whalers. Dorey is really another Maple Leaf loss to the rival league since he had committed to the WHA while still in Toronto.

Small scoring forward Guy Trottier also jumped to the new league with Ottawa while Mike Pelyk, Paul Henderson, and Dave Keon left over the next three years to join the WHA. The Leafs lost all these players for a few thousand dollars each but Leaf owner Harold Ballard would not compete with the new circuit. Other NHL teams were supposed to do as the Leafs were doing but the New York Rangers, for example, were determined not to lose anyone of consequence to the new league. Sittler was wooed heavily by the new league at one point but decided to stay with the Maple Leafs for less money.

Defenseman Rick Ley defends against Boston's Phil Esposito. (York University Archives/*Toronto Telegram* Collection)

How significant the players lost to the WHA is debatable (other than Parent) in many instances but the Leafs lost an incredible amount of depth and were unable to bring other players along more slowly. There is no doubt the 1972–73 season was one of the worst in Leaf history (only 27 wins) with the team forced to use many unproven and untried players (especially on defense with the likes of Joe Lundrigan, John Grisdale, Larry McIntyre and Dave Fortier). The Leafs improved drastically over the next few seasons but fans are still left to wonder how good the Leafs might have been if they could have kept all their players and not lost them for nothing in return—a theme too common in Leaf history since 1967.

65 Who Should Be Added to Legends Row

Previously Honoured:
September 2014—Johnny Bower, Darryl Sittler, Ted Kennedy
September 2015—Borje Salming, Mats Sundin
November 2015—Syl Apps, George Armstrong
October 2016—Turk Broda, Tim Horton, Dave Keon
October 2017—Wendel Clark, Charlie Conacher, Red Kelly, Frank Mahovlich

The Next Five:
Hap Day—Thirteen seasons as a player, with one Stanley Cup; 10 years as coach, with five Stanley Cups; and six seasons as general manager, with another Stanley Cup. Started with St. Pats and then became captain of the Leafs—28 years of exemplary service in the

Leaf organization. Elected to the Hockey Hall of Fame. A true "Leaf Lifer."

King Clancy—Colourful character, big part of the Leafs' 1932 Stanley Cup, played seven seasons with the Leafs, coached for three seasons in the '50s, was assistant general manager in the '60s with four Stanley Cups, in the organization for 42 years. Another "Leaf Lifer" and a member of the Hockey Hall of Fame.

Joe Primeau—"Gentleman Joe" was responsible for the success of the "Kid Line," and the 1932 Stanley Cup win. Starting in 1927, he played nine seasons with the Leafs, coached for three with a Stanley Cup. Elected to Hockey Hall of Fame and advisor to Conn Smythe into the late '50s. "True Blue" Leaf.

Conn Smythe—Without Conn Smythe, there might not be a Leaf franchise. Saved the team from moving to Philadelphia in 1927, ran the team until the late 1950s. Small in stature but a larger than life figure in Toronto.

Foster Hewitt—Made the Leafs popular across Canada and overseas during WWII with his radio broadcasts, then later on television. As much a Maple Leaf as any other in the organization.

66 Blaine Stoughton and Gord McRae

Maple Leafs owner Harold Ballard was often roundly criticized for the way he operated the team and it was usually well deserved. But there was one time where Ballard stepped up with a pile of money and it helped his team win a best-of-three playoff series.

The 1974–75 season was another year of disappointment for the Maple Leafs, who thought they might be a contender after a strong showing in the 1973–74 campaign which saw the team add many new faces to their lineup including Ian Turnbull, Bob Neely, Lanny McDonald, Borje Salming, Inge Hammarstrom, plus three new goalies Doug Favell, Eddie Johnston, and Dunc Wilson. Also added to the team for the '74–'75 season were veteran wingers Bill Flett and Gary Sabourin and a defenseman acquired from Philadelphia named Willie Brossart. Nothing seemed to work and there was plenty of dissension on the team who stumbled to a 31–33–16 record, good for 78 points and a playoff spot. The Leafs first-round opponent was the Los Angeles Kings who had only finished 27 points ahead of Toronto during the regular season.

The Leafs became so desperate during the season they turned the net over to Gord McRae a virtual unknown free agent signing from 1971 (after a college career at Michigan Tech) who had been toiling in the minors with Tulsa, Oklahoma, and Dallas. Yet the unassuming McRae played in 20 games and posted a respectable 10–3–6 mark with 3.22 goals against average. Toronto coach Red Kelly named McRae his starter for the opening game in Los Angeles (the only Leaf playoff game not shown on regular TV because the Academy Awards were scheduled to be shown on CBC the same night), but a good effort was wasted when the Kings scored in overtime on a goal by Mike Murphy to take the game by a 3–2 score.

Two nights later at Maple Leaf Gardens saw the Toronto club turn the same trick on the Kings with a 3–2 overtime win on a goal by winger Blaine Stoughton. The Leafs had acquired Stoughton from Pittsburgh in a trade for the sharp shooting Rick Kehoe but he was not nearly as prolific a goal scorer at this point although he did manage 23 tallies in '74–'75. "It was really the only second decent chance I had all night," Stoughton recounted. "Dave Keon made a super play for me. All I had to do was pull the trigger."

It was right after the game that Ballard came through for the Maple Leafs and their fans. The third and deciding game was to be played the very next night in Los Angeles, some 2,000 miles away. The Kings decided to stay overnight and fly commercial the

Toronto owner Harold Ballard. (Harold Barkley Archives)

next morning but Ballard paid in the neighborhood of $15,000 to charter a plane and get the team into Los Angeles at about 3:00 AM. Most observers at the time wondered if the Leafs would get any advantage of Ballard's efforts (the cost to the Kings on commercial craft was estimated to be around $4,000) but the Leaf owner would be vindicated this time.

Toronto jumped out to a 2–0 lead on goals by George Ferguson and Inge Hammarstrom and then held on for dear life behind the goaltending of McRae to eke out a 2–1 victory. On the front page of the *Toronto Star* the next day was a photo of Ballard about to kiss the cheek of his goalie as a gesture of thank you. Of course, it did not hurt that the team had just secured at least two more home playoff dates but Ballard did look good from all angles with his idea of getting the Leafs to Los Angeles as soon as possible.

The Leaf players spoke bravely about having to play the defending Stanley Cup champions in the next round but it was all to no avail. The Flyers rolled over the Leafs in four straight games and the final insult was watching Andre "Moose" Dupont clinch the best-of-seven with an overtime winner right in Maple Leaf Gardens on a Saturday night coast-to-coast television broadcast.

McRae was with the Leafs for three more seasons but was never relevant again, although he posted a respectable 30–22–10 record overall. Stoughton's stay as a Maple Leaf would be short but in 1979–80 he tied the league high mark of 56 goals for the Hartford Whalers who had just joined the NHL that season.

67 Worst Moves by Owner Harold Ballard

1. Taking over ownership of the team after his business partner Stafford Smythe passed away in 1971.
2. Convicted of tax fraud and had to serve a year in prison as a result.
3. Brought back Punch Imlach to run the Maple Leafs in 1979—an unmitigated disaster.
4. Did not let Dave Keon go to another NHL team despite not wanting to resign the four-time Stanley Cup champion.
5. Tried his best to embarrass coach Roger Neilson, including asking him to wear a paper bag over his head prior to a game.
6. Naming Gerry McNamara (1981), Gord Stellick (1988), and Floyd Smith (1989) as general managers of the team.
7. When captain Darryl Sittler asked for a contract adjustment, Ballard refused and started another feud.
8. Went through nine coaches during his tenure as Leafs owner from 1971 to 1990.
9. Spent money to buy the Hamilton Tiger-Cats of the CFL when he should have put that money into the hockey team.
10. Despite financial difficulties, he would never secure partners to bring in more money and help the team. Molson Breweries did loan Ballard millions of dollars, but that was a side deal kept quiet so he could still retain all his power as sole owner of the Maple Leafs.

68 Borje Salming

The Maple Leafs have never enjoyed much success playing against the Philadelphia Flyers since the team wearing orange and black entered the NHL starting with the 1967–68 season. In their first year of existence the Flyers beat the Leafs three times in four meetings and it has rarely improved for the Leafs since then.

It gets worse when the playoff meeting between the two teams is examined. The teams met for the first time in the postseason in 1975 and to put it bluntly the Flyers skated over the Maple Leafs in four consecutive games. The '75 series ended when defenseman Andre "Moose" Dupont scored an overtime winner at Maple Leaf Gardens with the assist going to Dave Schultz. The Flyers outscored the Leafs 15–6 over the four games and a rather weak Toronto team was never in the series. The Flyers were too big and too tough for the Leafs to make any sort of dent in the armour of a team that was going to win the Stanley Cup for the second consecutive season.

The playoff meeting between the two teams was different in 1976 and went the full seven games before the Flyers prevailed once again. The Leafs were a much tougher team in the '76 re-match after adding hard-nosed players like Pat Boutette, Scott Garland, Dave Dunn, Dave "Tiger" Williams and linebacker tough guy Kurt Walker to their lineup. It was an extremely physical series, and the Leafs gave all they had. The Philadelphia side never changed their approach under Hall of Fame coach Fred Shero and did not shy away from any invitation to fight.

Star defenseman Borje Salming of the Leafs was a constant target of the Flyers' attention with Mel Bridgman taking advantage of a moment when the Leafs had none of their tougher guys on the ice to lay a severe beating on the slick Swede. Salming was not a

Toronto defenseman Borje Salming (#21) is a member of the Hall of Fame.
(Robert Shaver)

fighter but managed to stay in the game despite getting pounded and the Leafs prevailed in the third contest 5–4 to get the Leafs back into the series. The next game saw Salming score a great goal on the Flyers Bernie Parent which brought a tremendous reaction from the Maple Leafs Gardens crowd in a 4–3 Leafs win. Salming's tally was one of the most memorable in team history and showed a great player cannot be beaten down.

Toronto captain Darryl Sittler tied a Stanley Cup record with five goals in the sixth contest (an 8–5 Leafs victory) which was another brutal game but the Leafs had no choice but to play this way or get steamrolled again. It was not enough to win the series in '76 (too many injuries and not enough scoring to win a game in Philadelphia), but the Leafs were no longer pushovers. The Flyers did not like the Leafs fighting back and it sapped them of vital energy when they played Montreal in the '76 Stanley Cup final (which turned out to be a sweep for the mighty Habs). The teams met again in the 1977 playoffs and this time the fighting was reduced to almost nothing. Toronto won the first two games right in Philadelphia and were coming home to the Gardens for the next two games. The Flyers ended up winning both in overtime even though the Leafs led both games late in regulation time. The Leafs did not recover and lost the series in six games. It was one of the most disappointing series losses in Leafs history and left many broken hearted to see the nasty Flyers win again.

Toronto has only beaten Philadelphia once in the postseason and it came with Leafs goalie Curtis Joseph putting on a great show in the 1999 playoffs. The Flyers however won the next two times the teams met in the postseason to bring their record to 6–1 versus Toronto when it matters most in hockey.

69 Is There a Goalie in the House?

Alfie Moore—April 5, 1938—Game 1 Finals—Chicago vs Toronto—MLG

The old saying applies here: "Don't let the facts get in the way of a good story." Legend says that injured Chicago goaltender Mike Karakas was replaced by minor league goaltender Alfie Moore, who was hauled out of a Toronto tavern. Prior to Game 1 of the finals, league president Frank Calder ruled that star New York Rangers goaltender Dave Kerr was ineligible to replace Karakas, and that Moore, who was the designated spare goalie, would have to tend goal. The pregame argument between the Chicago and Toronto brass was so heated that Conn Smythe and Hawks' coach Bill Stewart engaged in a fist fight!

Alfie Moore did play, and guarded the net so well that the Hawks beat the Leafs 3–1, with Chicago eventually winning the Stanley Cup in four games.

The tavern story?

A disgruntled Chicago reporter wrote that since Toronto thinks its the centre of the hockey universe (yes, even in 1938) that they can bring in any goalie, including one who had been drinking all afternoon.

Len Broderick—October 30, 1957—Montreal vs Toronto—MLG

Starting his third year with the Junior Marlies and just having passed his 18th birthday, Len Broderick was called on to replace the great Jacques Plante in the Montreal net. Plante had suffered an asthma attack. "Standby" goalie Broderick was alerted arriving at

Maple Leaf Gardens a mere half hour prior to the opening face-off. Dressing besides Maurice Richard, Jean Beliveau, Doug Harvey, and Bernie Geoffrion, to name a few of the stars, must have been intimidating. But also comforting, since these Habs were the reigning Stanley Cup champions.

Len Broderick allowed only two goals in a 6–2 victory for the Canadiens. And it so happened that the Parkhurst Company was present during this game, taking photos for the 1957–58 hockey card set and Broderick appeared in several action shots. Nice souvenir to remember his only NHL game.

Don Keenan—March 7, 1959—Boston vs Toronto—MLG
On March 7, 1959, the Leafs sat in last place with eight games to go, five points behind the fourth place New York Rangers, who had a game in hand with the Detroit Red Wings in between. Punch Imlach had taken on the coaching duties earlier that season, insisting that his team would make the playoffs despite what the "experts" were saying.

The Rangers beat the Hawks that afternoon and now the Leafs were seven points out. Bruin goaltender Harry Lumley would be only too happy to knock his former team out of the playoff race.

But old "Apple Cheeks" Lumley became ill that afternoon and the summons was out for 20-year-old Don Keenan to play goal. Keenan, who hadn't played a game that season and had only been on skates once in three weeks, was introduced to coach Boston coach Milt Schmidt by a smirking Punch Imlach.

The nervous youngster allowed four goals but performed well enough to be named third star of the game. The 4–1 victory kept the Leafs in the playoff race, eventually making the playoffs on the last night of the season—by a mere one point.

It was Don Keenan's only NHL game.

Dave Dryden—February 3, 1962—New York Rangers vs Toronto—MLG

Early in the second period of the February 3, 1962, game against the Rangers, Leaf captain George Armstrong scored on a fallen Gump Worsley. When the "Gumper" failed to get up, the call went out for "house goalie" Dave Dryden, goaltender for the Toronto Marlboros in the Metro Junior "A" League.

Unlike Broderick and Keenan, Dryden didn't get the benefit of actually meeting his new teammates until the second intermission. The older brother of Hall of Famer Ken Dryden played well and received quite the ovation from the crowd even though he gave up three goals to the Leafs who won by the score of 4-1.

Dave Dryden, however, did have a long and productive career in the NHL with Chicago, Buffalo, and Edmonton, and in the WHA with the Chicago Cougars and Edmonton Oilers.

David Ayers—February 22, 2020—Carolina vs Toronto—Scotiabank Arena

The term "15 minutes of fame" didn't apply to practice goalie and Zamboni driver David Ayers. In an astounding turn of events, both Carolina Hurricanes goaltenders were injured in a nationally televised game against the Leafs, with the Canes leading 4–1. Both teams were fighting for a playoff spot, so it was quite the predicament.

After a long delay, the 42-year-old emergency goalie appeared wearing No. 90. The overconfident Toronto players scored on their first two shots to come within one goal at the end of the second period. In the third period, not only did the Canes score twice but they put a blanket on the Leafs, with Ayers making eight saves for the victory over a now disheartened Leaf team.

For weeks after the game, Ayers appeared on many television and radio shows in Toronto and New York City and was being hailed as a hero in Raleigh, Carolina.

The Final Broadcast: Foster Hewitt

Foster Hewitt was an iconic figure in the hockey world starting in the 1920s with his radio broadcasts. His high-pitched voice was familiar to all hockey fans in the 1930s, 1940s and into the 1950s before the advent of the television version of *Hockey Night in Canada* in 1952. Not only was Foster remembered fondly for the excitement he provided by calling play by play of Toronto Maple Leaf games across Canada on cold Saturday nights in the winter, he was heard by Canadian servicemen overseas during WW II through his recorded broadcasts. The legendary Hewitt was an important part of morale boosting for Canadians at home and on the front lines abroad. Most of all Hewitt is remembered as one of the pioneers of hockey broadcasting and he coined many phrases which are still used in hockey play-by-play descriptions today.

In those radio days Foster was in the gondola in Maple Leaf Gardens calling the game solo. There was no "colour man" or analyst in the booth, and there was never the thought of having one. But listening to recordings of radio games from the '40s, it's apparent that Foster, while calling the action, also had a knack of analyzing the play as well. Foster really gave a complete sense of how the game was unfolding. And, in those pre-television days, when it was necessary to get an off-ice account of some incident that might warrant a suspension, it was Foster Hewitt who was consulted—his grasp of the game was that well respected.

He was also so popular with Canadians across the country, that during a train trip across the prairies with the famed Maple Leafs of the 1930s, Foster often garnered more attention than the players—much to the amusement of stars like Red Horner. And, when a pre-teen Bobby Hull actually met Foster Hewitt in person after being fascinated by listening to Leaf games on radio, the future superstar exclaimed, "I looked up and it felt like I was looking at God!" Such was the attraction of Foster Hewitt and his radio broadcasts, and the popularity of the Maple Leafs grew and grew. By 1951 the Maple Leafs had racked up seven Stanley Cups and with 13 trips to the final since 1927.

Naturally, when television came along, Foster was the obvious choice to be the first to call Leaf games on Saturday nights on CBC. The TV games were simulcast on radio and this continued until the start of the 1958–59 season. At that point a significant change was revealed to the television audience when Foster Hewitt, just after his usual opening, announced: "This season, play by play for radio and TV, I'm very proud to say, will be handled by my son Bill Hewitt. After 30 years of play by play, my efforts will be interjecting highlights and comments during the course of play." Thus, history was made on October 11, 1958 with Foster handing over the microphone to the first new personality calling a Leaf game since 1931, and the "colour analyst" was born!

Young Bill Hewitt had a tough act to follow for sure and the "living legend" would be right over his shoulder. But Bill, who had been calling junior games from the gondola during the '50s had already experienced action from the booth on "Young Canada Night" (a long-forgotten tradition) starting when he was eight years old. The arrangement with Bill calling the games and Foster doing the colour lasted for two seasons when the elder Hewitt went back to solely calling the games on radio. It wasn't until the 1963–64 season when a rotation of newspapermen provided analyses on the television broadcasts beside Bill. The younger Hewitt had no chance to be as impactful as his father but he was terrific at capturing the action and made the transition very easy for everyone—especially the fans. The debut of Bill on national TV in October of 1958 was the start of the Toronto Maple Leaf dynasty of the 1960s and four Stanley Cups. Maybe Bill was a good luck charm as well.

As for Foster he continued on radio (appearing on *Hockey Night in Canada* at the end of games to help with analysis and the three-star selection), but by the 1970s he was mostly doing home games only. Eventually he was replaced by Ron Hewat (one of Foster's employees at his radio station 1430 CKFH) for play-by-play duties. But on the night of November 15, 1978 the 75-year-old Foster came back to call a game on television for one last time. The Leafs and Sabres played a 2–2 tie and Foster's appearance was a celebration of the 47th anniversary of the first game he broadcast out of the Gardens on November 12, 1931. By all accounts Foster was just as sharp as he had been for all eight games of the 1972 Summit Series. And, he used his trademark description "He shoots, he scores" to call the first goal of the game. A fitting way to end a legendary career!

71 Best TV Commercial Using Maple Leaf Players

Over the years Maple Leaf players have always been sought out to help promote a variety of services and products (not to mention a host of charitable causes or functions). Getting endorsements from Toronto hockey stars is a surefire way to bring attention to a product or service and that will likely always be the case. Some of these endorsements end up as television commercials and one of the most memorable of these came in 1978 when forward Lanny McDonald and defenseman Brian Glennie combined for a 30 second spot.

The scene opens with both players entering a kitchen and Glennie rips the freezer door off a refrigerator because he wants his Swanson's Hungry Man Dinner. McDonald says Glennie goes wild to tame his big appetite while the beefy defenseman explains what different types of Hungry Man Dinners are available. The commercial concludes with the two players agreeing that the dinners "can turn a wild man into a pussycat." McDonald finishes the dialogue with the word "meow" and both players let out a hearty chuckle. The commercial is available on YouTube for viewing.

The 1977–78 season was the final one the two players would spend together on the Leafs team. Glennie had first joined the Maple Leafs in 1969 while McDonald was a highly touted number one draft choice (4th overall) in 1973 and made the Leafs for the 1973–74 season. The team was moderately successful between '73 and '77, but had a breakthrough year in 1977–78 under rookie coach Roger Neilson. The '77–'78 Maple Leafs won 41 games and finished with 92 points in the regular season. McDonald scored 47

Lanny McDonald scores the series winner in overtime against the New York Islanders. (AP Images)

goals (the most of any player on the team) while Glennie enjoyed one of his best years with 17 points in 77 games played and a plus/minus rating of plus 24.

The Leafs wiped out the Los Angeles Kings in two straight games to win the preliminary round of the '78 postseason but then had to face the heavily favoured New York Islanders in the next round. The Isles took the first two games at home (one in overtime on a goal by Mike Bossy) but the Leafs won both their home games to even the series. The fifth game back in New York also went into extra time but ended when Islander forward Bob Nystrom went around Glennie at the Maple Leaf blueline and scored to give the home side a 2–1 win and put Toronto on the brink of elimination. The inconsolable Leaf defenseman blamed himself for the winning goal. However, the Leafs came back strong in the sixth game at home to beat the Isles 5–2 and force a seventh game.

The last game of a very physical series was close all the way and went into overtime tied 1–1. The Maple Leafs caught a great break when McDonald was able to take an Ian Turnbull pass at the Islander blueline before breaking in on New York goalie Glenn Resch. McDonald let go his great wrist shot and it went into the far side of the net to give the Leafs a 2–1 win and the series. The goal was very significant for the Maple Leafs since it meant that they had won a best-of-seven series for the first time since 1964.

As McDonald basked in the hero's glow, Glennie revealed that he kept a seashell in his jock for good luck. It worked out well for the rugged rearguard who no longer had to worry about his mistake in the previous overtime game haunting him. The underdog Maple Leafs proved they were nobody's pussycats in this series. Meow!

Glennie was traded away before the start of the next season while McDonald was dealt before 1979 was over.

72 Best TV Commercials Involving the Maple Leafs

1. **Lanny McDonald** and **Brian Glennie** promoting Hungry Man frozen dinners.
2. Montreal Canadiens goalie is obsessed with Leafs captain **Mats Sundin** in a series of Nike commercials.
3. **Wendel Clark** promotes Chunky Soup while running over opposing players.
4. **Eddie Shack's** Pop Shoppe commercials where he has "a nose for value."
5. **Mats Sundin** and **Wayne Gretzky** trying to outdo each other with trick shots for McDonalds.

73 Mats Sundin

All Maple Leaf fans were shocked on the night of June 28, 1994, when beloved captain Wendel Clark was traded by Toronto to the Quebec Nordiques in exchange for Mats Sundin. There were other players in the deal but the main two were Clark and Sundin and Toronto fans were never really happy about the six-player trade (there were draft choices involved as well).

While it was indeed a shock to lose the feisty leadership of Clark, the Leafs were getting back one of the most talented players in all of hockey who had been drafted first overall in 1989. Sundin had been very productive for the Nordiques but they had so many young players on their roster (mostly as a result of drafting high up at the

Entry Draft for a number of years) that they were not going to pay a high price to keep all of them. Quebec management decided they would sacrifice Sundin if they could get the right deal and when Clark was made available, they quickly decided to make the trade.

Cliff Fletcher was the Maple Leafs general manager at the time and he was never one to shy away from a big deal. He felt the '93–'94 Leafs had gone as far as they could and needed some young blood to revamp their attack. Sundin could shoot, score, set up plays and play game in and game out—something Clark could not do with his back problems. Sundin became a consistent point producer and goal scorer over his 13 years as a Maple Leaf yet he could not take them to the Stanley Cup.

It would be unfair if it was not pointed out that Sundin did not have a consistent winger on his side who could score—a big issue that the Maple Leafs never solved although many were tried. Sadly, they traded away winger Fredrik Modin just as he was ready to blossom and that took away a potential great line mate from Sundin. The Leafs also brought in a variety of second line centres to play behind their Swedish captain but once again none ever worked out for the team.

With Sundin on the team, the Maple Leafs were in contention more often than not, but could only reach the Conference final level on two occasions and got beat by teams they should have been able to handle (especially Carolina in the 2002 postseason). The Leafs made sure Sundin was paid handsomely and gave the big Swede (6'5", 231 pounds) what he wanted in terms of no-trade or movement clauses as time moved along. Sundin rewarded Toronto fans by becoming the franchise's all-time leader in goals (420) and points (987). Maple Leafs fans rejoiced with Sundin when he scored his 500th career goal to beat Calgary 5–4 in overtime during the 2006–07 season. It was a three-goal night for Sundin on October 14, 2006 with the final goal coming in overtime with the Maple Leafs short-handed!

Toronto captain Mats Sundin (Dennis Miles)

However, the next season of 2007–08 was not a good one for Toronto and it was obvious the Maple Leafs were not going to make the postseason (again), so management went to Sundin with trade options. He turned them all down saying that he did not want to go to another team late in the season even if they would go on to win the Stanley Cup. Sundin reasoned that he would not feel he was part of any team if he had not been there the whole year.

While Sundin was entitled to his point of view, it was odd to say the least. It denied the Maple Leafs a chance to pick up much needed assets like prospects and draft choices. A few of his teammates also declined to be traded (Darcy Tucker, Tomas Kaberle, and Pavel Kubina to name a few) and the now acting general manager of the Maple Leafs, the same Cliff Fletcher who had brought Sundin to Toronto, was left fuming although he did not direct any criticism to his captain.

Not only did Sundin refuse a trade, he also declined to sign a new deal. He would eventually sign a new deal with Vancouver the mid-way through the following season (so much for being with a team the whole way!) and came back to Toronto and scored the winning goal for the Canucks in a shootout at the ACC. Sundin retired after Vancouver's failed run in the 2009 postseason but Leaf fans were left to wonder what if the former captain had agreed to be traded to another team. Would the Maple Leafs have been that much better off? The return on a deal for Sundin would likely have been significant but Maple Leaf fans would never know for sure.

If there were any lingering bad feelings, they were all gone by 2012—a year that saw Sundin's sweater number 13 lifted to the rafters at the Air Canada Centre and his induction into the Hockey Hall of Fame. Time had passed and though not all the wounds might have healed, the man who captained the team for 776 regular season games was not going to be denied his rightful place in team history.

74 Best Maple Leaf Biography: Dave "Tiger" Williams

The Maple Leafs are one of the most chronicled clubs in professional sports with a wide variety of books looking at the history of the fabled blue and white over many years. While most of the books that cover the existence of the Maple Leafs since 1927 are usually very well done and quite informative, biographies of players, coaches, managers, and owners are the recommended read for Toronto hockey fans who want to learn about the lives of some of the most colourful characters in the history of hockey.

One of the very best biographies done about a Maple Leaf player is entitled *Tiger: A Hockey Story* written by former Toronto tough guy Dave Williams along with writer James Lawton. Published in 1986 with Williams at the end of his career, the popular Leaf winger delivers a no holds barred account of his life as an NHL player. His time as a Maple Leaf is clearly described with Williams letting loose on everyone he thought deserved to be exposed. Williams and his co-author are not really mean but brutally honest and the truculent hockey player does not hesitate to name names. The book is not a long tome (only 172 pages) but the impact is much like a Tiger body check or fight—right in your face.

It should come as no surprise that a book written in conjunction with Williams would come across in a straight forward manner. As a youngster in Grade 9, Williams wrote "NHL" for his ambition on a career guidance form. There was no doubt what he wanted to do with his life. After a good junior career in Swift Current, Saskatchewan (which included a 52-goal season in 1973–74), the Maple Leafs selected the 5'11", 190-pound left winger with the choppy skating stride 31st overall in 1974. He played briefly in the minors before the Leafs called him up during the 1974–75 season.

Toronto legendary tough guy Dave "Tiger" Williams. (Robert Shaver)

On January 18, 1975 Williams scored his first NHL goal against the Montreal Canadiens at the Forum. The Leafs were down 3–2 but tied when Williams took a pass from captain Darryl Sittler in the slot and snapped a shot past Michel Larocque to even the score. Tiger did a dance to celebrate his first ever big-league tally and he knew he was in the big league to stay. The ever-confident Williams said afterward, "I'm glad it was a good clean goal, not a tip in or deflection. I saw the upper shelf open and put a wrist shot right there." He was a Maple Leaf until February of 1980 and the Toronto club missed his spirited approach to the game after he was dealt to Vancouver. Williams would go on to play in 962 NHL games while scoring 241 goals for five teams before retiring after the 1987–88 season. More notably he ended his career as the NHL's all-time bad boy with 3,966 penalty minutes. Considering his wide and varied career it is no wonder his book is one of the most interesting volumes ever written about the game. Tiger's unique perspective is well worth the time to investigate.

75 Maple Leaf Biographies

Hockey Is a Battle—Leaf coach George "Punch" Imlach gives his side of the story between 1958 and 1969.

Open Ice—The career of Leaf defenseman Tim Horton is examined in detail.

The Big M—Leaf superstar Frank Mahovlich covers his entire NHL career with Toronto, Detroit, and Montreal.

Over the Boards—Leaf winger Ron Ellis discusses his hockey triumphs and his difficulties away from the game.

Lowering the Boom—Toronto defenseman Bobby "Boomer" Baun takes the reader through his entire career.

More Recent Titles

Bower: A Legendary Life—A comprehensive account of the 'China Wall'

Eddie Shack: Hockey's Most Entertaining Stories—as told by Eddie himself

Bleeding Blue: Giving My All for the Game—Wendell Clark's own story

Killer: My Life in Hockey—Doug Gilmour's story—another fan favourite

The Red Kelly Story—One of the all-time best players

Other Maple Leaf Biographies:

Conn Smythe, Harold Ballard, Foster Hewitt, Bill Barilko, Ted Kennedy, Turk Broda, Max Bentley, Borje Salming, Howie Meeker, King Clancy, Danny Lewicki, Lanny McDonald, Terry Sawchuk, Brian Conacher, Carl Brewer, Curtis Joseph, Tie Domi, Tiger Williams, Darryl Sittler, Paul Henderson, Mirko Frycer

76 The Night Wayne Gretzky Got Rocked

It was often said that Wayne Gretzky had eyes in the back of his head during his entire NHL career. Blessed with great peripheral vision, the "Great One" rarely got hit because he could see everything out on the ice. It was also said (without any verification) that there was some sort of unofficial rule that Gretzky was not to be hit but on the night of January 3, 1981, one Leaf player decided he would break the rule, real or otherwise.

Bill McCreary was a strapping 6', 190-pound American born winger the Maple Leafs had drafted 114th overall in 1979 after he had played at Colgate University for one season. The Leafs liked McCreary's bloodlines (his father, Bill Sr., had played in the NHL with the St. Louis Blues and his uncle, Keith, also played in the big league) and assigned him to the New Brunswick team in the American Hockey League for the '80–'81 season. He got called up to the Leafs on December 30ᵗʰ and played his first game against the St. Louis Blues, a 5–3 road loss by the Leafs.

Toronto's five game road trip continued into the New Year with a Saturday contest in Edmonton. The Leafs lost the game 4–1 but all the talk was McCreary's late third period hit on Gretzky which flattened the Edmonton superstar right on his back. The Oiler centre was coming across the Maple Leaf blueline going left to right with his head down somewhat as he tried to corral the puck. McCreary was coming in the exact opposite direction straight up and unloaded a hard hit which rocked Gretzky quite visibly. He went down to his knees and then lay on his back with his gloves off, looking up at the arena ceiling for a few minutes until he received medical attention and caught his breath.

By the standards of the time the check was clean and no Oiler attacked McCreary although threatening words were directed toward the Leaf rookie. There was no penalty on the play and really no complaint from Gretzky who was known as a bit of a whiner during the early days of his career (this game was played during Gretzky's second year in the NHL). "I got a little careless, left myself open and he (McCreary) caught me a good one," Gretzky said after the game which saw the Edmonton star record three points (1G, 2A). "It was my own fault," he concluded. For his part McCreary said, "It was a clean hit and he sort of ran into me going pretty fast. He didn't see me and if I wanted to put some elbow and stick into it, I could have hurt him. But I don't play that way."

The solid jolt to the Oilers top player did not seem to inspire the Leafs (who would finish the year with just 28 wins) in any way, but McCreary did score his first and only NHL goal (assisted by

Darryl Sittler and Wilf Paiement) the next night in Calgary during an 8–5 Maple Leaf loss to the Flames. McCreary played a total of 12 games recording only one point for the Leafs and spent most of '80–'81 in the minors. He never returned to Toronto or the NHL after that season and played out his career in the minor leagues where he scored 30 goals on two occasions for the Milwaukee Admirals who played in the now defunct International Hockey League.

Gretzky was never hit in such a thunderous manner again because he learned to keep his head up and he became one of the most protected players in NHL history. Gretzky can probably thank McCreary and his body check for that reality which had a major impact on his ability to notch 61 NHL records before he retired in 1999.

McCreary's professional hockey career was over by the time he was 28 years old but at least he had one brief shining moment in the spotlight when his steamroller check on Wayne Gretzky made history.

77 Leaf Nation— Out of This World

Foster Hewitt's Saturday night broadcast of Leaf games was a regular staple for hockey fans. Those fans across Canada became Leaf fans. "Hello Canada and Hockey Fans in the United States and Newfoundland" was Foster's opening greeting. During World War II, Foster added, "and an extra hello to servicemen overseas." There were Leaf fans all over the world. But how about fans "out of this world?"

On January 21, 2013, there was a special ceremonial puck drop at the Air Canada Centre prior to a game between the Buffalo Sabres and the Toronto Maple Leafs. Astronaut Chris Hadfield simulated an extra-terrestrial event. The first Canadian to command the International Space Station was shown greeting Leaf fans and dropping the puck from the ISS. The brilliant feature involving Leaf alumni had Felix Potvin catching the puck from space, handing it to Darcy Tucker in the bowels of the ACC, who in turn passed it over to Darryl Sittler, who then raced up to ice level to Johnny Bower, who completed the ceremonial puck drop from space to the huge ovation of fans in the rink and undoubtedly across the country.

It was certainly well-choreographed, and the famous Canadian astronaut is truly a devoted Leaf fan. During his two-hour workout on the treadmill in the space capsule, instead of seeing the world from 409,000 meters above the ground, he viewed Leaf games that were uploaded from earth.

As for the puck drop, Hadfield's first attempt was a failure, as the disc just floated. Zero gravity can do that. He then propelled the puck downward, ostensibly to the waiting gloved hand of former Leaf netminder Felix Potvin.

But there was a hitch. There was no actual hockey puck on board the space station. One of the Hadfield's crew members, a Russian cosmonaut, saved the day by suggesting that his black camera lens cap could do the trick. It worked. And no one knew otherwise.

Like most Canadian youngsters. Hadfield grew up watching *Hockey Night in Canada* on Saturday nights, with Dave Keon as his favourite player. The Hadfield family had talked about a long-ago connection to the Leafs and owner Conn Smythe. But information was scarce. It was thought that Chris' grandfather Sgt. Major Austin Hadfield had been the Leafs' trainer in the 1930s. But Tim

Canadian astronaut Chris Hadfield seeking information on his family's link to his beloved Maple Leafs at Mike Wilson's "Ultimate Leafs Fan" museum.
(Photo courtesy Event Imaging)

Daly held that job. And there was only one team trainer. Maybe it was just a wild story.

Hockey historians Paul Patskou and Mike Wilson took on the task of assisting the Hadfield family in their search for confirmation. They discovered that not only was Sgt. Hadfield associated with the Leafs in the mid-30s but he may have been the first physical training instructor in hockey. Smythe thought that if anyone could get his "Gashouse Gang" of players in shape, it would be an army drillmaster. Charlie Conacher, Red Horner, and others were more into "fun" than training. That changed. The Sgt. Major was tough!

Smythe, a military man, would have heard of Hadfield, who was stationed in Galt with the Highland Light Infantry Regiment. He needed an edge for his team and thought conditioning was the answer to be led by a man with a reputation for driving his recruits hard.

Smythe warned goaltender George Hainsworth and the others that they "better come in shape; you're in for a surprise." At 7:00 AM, Hadfield indeed put them through an hour of physical torture. The players couldn't challenge Hadfield, who was described to the readers as "a huge-chested martinet with army regulations written all over his frame." Hadfield had the players carry each other on their backs, well before the Russians did. The players called Hadfield "Joe Palooka" after a fictional boxer—behind his back of course.

At the Leafs' training camp in the 1970s, the players did challenge the PT instructor, professional wrestler Fred Atkins, who was over 60 years of age at the time. Atkins put all those challengers flat on their backs.

Chris Hadfield, the Canadian astronaut and rabid Leaf fan, can say that one of his greatest thrills was going up in space and having the Leaf logo floating around in the ISS. But he is also proud of his familial connection to his beloved Toronto Maple Leafs. When Patskou and Wilson presented their research to Chris, he responded: "There's always a difference between family lore and reality…. You always have that feeling: 'Did this story grow over time?' But it's so delightful to see it's all true."

78 A New Year's Eve to Remember

The 1981–82 edition of the Maple Leafs was one of the worst teams ever in franchise history which gave Toronto fans little to cheer for over the entire 80-game schedule. However, the rag-tag club had a sort of special evening for a few youngsters as the calendar year for 1981 came to a close.

The Leafs were in Detroit on New Year's Eve for a contest against the equally wretched Red Wings with an injury depleted lineup. The Leaf defense featured youngsters Bob McGill, Barry Melrose, Fred Boimistruck, and Jim Benning, but their best two blueliners, Borje Salming and Bob Manno, were both out with injuries. Craig Muni (selected 25th overall in 1980) and Darwin McCutcheon (selected 179th overall in '80) from the Windsor Spitfires of the OHL were both called up as replacements and played in their first ever NHL contest.

Up front, the Leafs also had a number of players out which gave a chance to centre Fred Perlini (chosen 158th overall in '80), a member of the junior Toronto Marlboros. This game would mark Perlini's second NHL contest having played the night before in Toronto against the St. Louis Blues when he recorded one assist on a goal by Terry Martin. Also added up front was centre Norm Aubin (selected 51st overall in 1979) although he saw little ice time.

Luckily the Leafs had veteran goalie Michel "Bunny" Larocque in net and he was fantastic in stopping 48 of 50 Detroit shots to backstop the Toronto side to a 5–2 victory. The Leafs only got 21 shots on Detroit goalie Bob Sauve but received goals from veterans Rocky Saganiuk, Bill Derlago, Wilf Paiement, and Rick Vaive to help lead the attack. The other goal was scored by Perlini, his first NHL marker and he also earned an assist on Saganiuk's opening tally. Perlini's goal was set up nicely by winger Rene Robert who gave him a pass that only needed to be redirected into an open net. "It's a thrill to be here with the team," Perlini said after the game. "I'm really happy about how things are going."

Muni did not make the score sheet but coach Mike Nykoluk was impressed with his imposing size (listed at 6', 200 pounds) and how he played his defensive position. McCutcheon was given a minor penalty (for delay of game) and limited ice time as Nykoluk mused about how the large youngster (6', 190 pounds) might need more seasoning. McCutcheon wore sweater number two and got his picture in the paper while he was knocking down Detroit forward Derek Smith in front of the Leaf net. The win was the 11th of the season for the Leafs and gave them a total of 31 points as 1982 began, a mere five points ahead of the Red Wings who were mired in the basement of the six-team Norris Division. Toronto trailed the Winnipeg Jets by three points but held two games in hand. Despite the New Year's Eve win the Leafs would go on to finish '81–'82 with just 20 wins and well out of the playoff picture.

Muni would go on to play just 19 games for the Leafs before going to Edmonton and sharing in three Stanley Cup wins with the Oilers. He would play in 819 regular season games over his entire NHL career. McCutcheon would never play another game for the Leafs or in the NHL but did play university hockey before playing minor league hockey in the AHL and the IHL. Perlini's career with Toronto lasted just eight games despite notching five points (2G, 3A). He would play in the minors for some time before heading to play in Europe. He put back-to-back 103 goal seasons while playing in Britain. Perlini is also the last Leaf player to play two games in one day. On the afternoon of February 20, 1982 he played a matinee contest at Maple Leaf Gardens with the Marlboros (scoring a goal and adding two assists in a 6–1 win over Oshawa) and then joined the Leafs in the evening for their game (going pointless) during an 8–5 win by the Leafs over the St. Louis

Toronto's Norm Aubin (#24) watches St. Louis forward Bernie Federko (#24).
(Robert Shaver)

Blues. He then played the next afternoon (making it three games in less than 24 hours) and had two assists in a Marlboros 4–1 win over Belleville.

Aubin would go on to play in 69 NHL career games (all with the Maple Leafs) but he would record a respectable 31 points (including 18 goals) over that time span. He then played in the minors for a number of seasons including a 47-goal campaign for the St. Catharines Saints, the Leafs farm team, in 1983–84.

December 31, 1981 in a Maple Leaf uniform will be a day four players will always remember even if their respective hockey careers went in varied directions from that day forward.

79 A Game the Leafs Should Have Lost

On the night of April 2, 1988, the Maple Leafs hosted the Detroit Red Wings on the final night of the regular season. Toronto needed to win this game to ensure they had a chance at a playoff spot during a turtle derby with the equally inept Minnesota North Stars. A win by the Leafs would give Toronto 52 points which would put them one ahead of Minnesota in the race for the final playoff spot in the Norris Division. The North Stars would play their final game in Calgary the next day so the Leafs would have to wait to find out their final fate, but a loss would end their season for certain.

The Red Wings under coach Jacques Demers stormed out to a 3–0 lead in the first period and looked to have the game well in hand. Toronto coach John Brophy switched goalies by taking Ken Wregget out and inserting Allan Bester in his place. The Leafs held Detroit off the rest of the opening stanza and then scored twice (on goals by Gary Leeman and Ed Olczyk) to make it 3–2 going into the final frame. Bester meanwhile was outstanding making great stops on Red Wing drives from Brent Ashton, Adam Oates, Jim Nill, Bob Probert and Gerard Gallant. The revitalized Leafs came on strong in the third and got goals from Tom Fergus (who netted two in the final frame) and one from Vincent Damphousse to win the game 5–3. Calgary beat Minnesota the next day and the Leafs had their playoff spot assured.

After the game Brophy said he had no choice but to turn to Bester who had not started a game since February 1st. "I had to do something to try to turn it around and get some life going," the white-haired coach said. The 27 save performance by Bester brought the diminutive netminder's career record against Detroit to 10–4–3. "I just wanted to go in there tonight to do well, to finish my season as best I could if things did not work out for us," Bester said. The Leafs goalie never lacked confidence or ego which rubbed some the wrong way (especially Wregget), but his overall record as a Leaf (61–91–16) never quite matched his bravado.

Often disliked for his high tempered approach to coaching, Brophy just wanted to take something out of a dismal season but he knew the chances of the Leafs advancing in the postseason were rather small. "If we are fortunate enough to get in, we're even with the Red Wings (the first-round opponent) and we will give them our best shot." The Leafs "best effort" included a humiliating 8–0 loss on home ice in the fourth game of the series that ranks as one of the worst in franchise history. For his part Fergus was never a Brophy booster (he very much disliked the coach's communication style which generally featured some screaming) and his goals to give the Leaf coach a playoff spot seem ironic to say the least. Everyone was happy for one night with a comeback win over the Red Wings.

However, it would have been much better if the Leafs had lost that game since it would have meant they would get the first choice in the 1988 NHL Entry Draft. Instead it went to the North Stars who selected centre Mike Modano (who was elected to the Hockey

Hall of Fame in 2014) with the choice. The next pick was Trevor Linden and he was the heart and soul of the Vancouver Canucks for many years. Either player would have helped the Leafs much more than three playoff dates in the 1988 postseason. The Leafs had many young players they had already drafted (Wendel Clark, Al Iafrate, Luke Richardson, Leeman, and Damphousse to name a few) and Modano or Linden would have fit in perfectly. Instead the Leafs picked winger Scott Pearson who ultimately delivered little to the Toronto cause. Once again, the Leafs missed out on a golden opportunity to improve their team in the long run.

In October of 2013 many of the Leaf players from the 1987–88 team visited Brophy in a Nova Scotia nursing home. Some of the visitors included Al Iafrate and Tom Fergus, players Brophy was hardest on during his tenure as Maple Leafs coach. The former taskmaster of the Leafs, now rather frail but still with his white thatch of hair, was brought to tears by the surprise visit by his former players.

80 Steve Thomas

Like many other NHL teams, the Maple Leafs have had their fair share of good and bad free agent signings over the years. Free agency was not even an issue until the 1980s when teams started looking at other ways to fill out their rosters as the league was now up to 21 teams. Players who were not drafted (many were from the junior or college ranks and some came from Europe) were a good source to fill out roster needs at both the big-league level and in the minors as well. While some Leaf fans might argue that Borje Salming was the best ever free agent signed by the team, the super

Swede came to the Maple Leafs in 1973 which makes the Hall of Fame defenseman more of an anomaly for his time frame. A better choice for the start of the true free agency period would be winger Steve Thomas.

Thomas was born in England but raised in Markham, Ontario, where he would star for the Markham Waxers, one of the best-known local teams. At the age of 18 Thomas scored 68 times during

Steve Thomas (Dennis Miles)

the 1981–82 season. That performance earned Thomas a spot on the Toronto Marlboros of the OHA and his final season saw him score 51 times and total 105 points in just 70 games played. The 20-year-old Thomas was still undrafted by any NHL team but the Maple Leafs decided to give a local kid a chance and put his name on a contract on May 12, 1984. Thomas was not a big man at 5'10" tall but he was a stocky 185 pounds and that earned him the nickname "Stumpy." He also had a rocket of a shot which was usually very accurate and he was not afraid of rough play.

Assigned to the minors for the 1984–85 campaign, Thomas scored 42 goals for the St. Catharines Saints of the American Hockey League and took home rookie of the year honours. He was back in St. Catharines the next season but 32 points in 19 games got him promoted to the Maple Leafs in 1985–86 where he scored 20 goals and totaled 57 points in 65 games played. Thomas scored 35 goals the following season and then promptly got into a contract dispute with the Leafs who felt compelled to trade him and Rick Vaive to Chicago. It was a very foolish move on the part of the Maple Leafs.

For the next 12 seasons, Thomas was generally a model of consistency while playing for the Chicago Blackhawks, New York Islanders, and the New Jersey Devils. Then in 1998 the Maple Leafs were able to bring back the scoring winger as a free agent and Thomas picked up 28 tallies playing alongside captain Mats Sundin. He was with the Leafs for three seasons before they once again decided he was not worth keeping. Thomas ended up on the Anaheim team that went to the seventh game of the Stanley Cup final against the Devils in 2003. Winning the Cup would have capped off a great career but Thomas would have to be content with scoring 421 career goals and recording 933 points in 1,235 games—not bad for a guy nobody wanted back in 1984!

Thomas had a great moment in his second stint with the Maple Leafs when he scored an overtime winning goal against Ottawa at the Air Canada Centre during the 2000 playoffs. Thomas redirected a pass behind Senators netminder Tom Barrasso to give the Leafs a 2–1 victory. His after-the-game comments were interesting. "I was fearful when I signed here. I knew there'd be a lot of pressure with people saying 'why would you sign a 34-year-old player?' I use that to fuel myself. I didn't want to look bad in front of everybody. I don't think there's any better place to play hockey than Toronto when you're successful."

Thomas' complete Maple Leaf record (118 G, 173A), shows he played in 377 games for the blue and white—a record that would be much higher had the Leafs held on to one of the best free agents they ever signed!

81 Best Free Agent Signings by the Maple Leafs Since 1980

1. **John Tavares**—Star centreman signs in July 2018 while still in his prime.
2. **Curtis Joseph**—Gave the Leafs great goaltending for four seasons after Felix Potvin faltered.
3. **Gary Roberts**—A heart-and-soul type who gave the Leafs some excellent play and leadership between 2000 and 2004.
4. **Steve Thomas**—A quality player who should have been a Maple Leaf his whole career.
5. **Alex Mogilny**—The most talented free agent the Leafs have ever added to their team and he won the Lady Byng Trophy in 2003.
6. **Ed Belfour**—Stepped into the Leafs net after Joseph left for Detroit and won 93 regular season games.

Goaltender Curtis Joseph (Dennis Miles)

7. **Tyler Bozak**—College free agent was one of the few free agent signings that worked out well for Brian Burke.

8. **Mike Johnson**—Never drafted but scored 20 goals one year and helped land Darcy Tucker in a trade.

9. **Clarke MacArthur**—Nice pick up from Atlanta who recorded 125 points in 195 games played.

10. **Gary Valk**—Scored overtime winner versus Pittsburgh in 1999 and was a good role player for the Leafs.

82 Best Leaf Farm Team Since the 1960s

The start of the 1991–92 season brought about a major change for the Maple Leafs main farm team. No longer a viable operation in Newmarket, Ontario (located north of Toronto) with poor attendance, the Leafs were enticed to move their farm team to St. John's Newfoundland—about as far away from Toronto as possible and still be in Canada. It was quite a move distance wise but there was an Atlantic Division in the American Hockey League at the time featuring other maritime cities like Moncton, Fredericton (both in New Brunswick), Halifax, and Cape Breton (both in Nova Scotia). The Leafs joined this division for the '91–'92 season not knowing quite what to expect and not anticipating much from their team since they had finished so poorly the previous year (26–45–9) under coach Frank Anzalone.

Marc Crawford was brought in to coach and veteran defenseman Joel Quenneville (a one-time Maple Leaf player) was named a playing assistant coach. Under their leadership the St. John's team racked up 90 points (39–29–12), good enough for second place in their division. The team had an interesting mix of youngsters and veterans in the lineup as is often the case in the minor leagues. The Leafs proceeded to beat Cape Breton in the opening round of the playoffs in just five games before sweeping the Moncton Hawks in the next round and winning their division in the postseason. The Leafs earned a bye to the AHL final where they would host the Adirondack Red Wings for the Calder Cup.

The final series went the distance and featured the road team winning every single game. The Red Wings took the first two games in Newfoundland but St. John's won twice on the road as well by scores of 4–3 and 4–1. The Red Wings took the next game in St. John's but the Maple Leafs secured a 5–2 road win to force a deciding game at home. However, a four goal third period did the St. John's club in with former Toronto goalie Allan Bester making 45 saves for the Adirondack club in the final contest. It was as far as any Maple Leaf farm team had advanced since the glory days of the Rochester Americans in the 1960s.

As disappointing as the final game was for the St. John's club, they could take solace in the knowledge that they were developing NHL players for the Maple Leafs. The star of the team was goalie Felix Potvin who went on to have a very good career in Toronto. Fellow netminder Damian Rhodes would also play for the Leafs as did Kent Manderville, Rob Pearson, Mike Eastwood, Drake Berehowsky, Guy Larose, and Yanic Perreault. Outside of Potvin none of these players turned into major stars, but it is still an impressive group that went on to play in the NHL. Others on the team also made a few appearances in a Leaf uniform but the most success awaited coaches Crawford and Quenneville who between them have won three Stanley Cups as head coaches.

The St. John's team was never as good again and would eventually return to Toronto in 2005 to play out of the Ricoh Coliseum located just a few minutes away from the Air Canada Centre. The team was renamed "Marlies" (in tribute to a name synonymous with junior hockey success in Toronto) and the team made it to

Goaltender Felix Potvin (Dennis Miles)

the AHL final in 2011–12. Some of the more impressive performers for the Marlies that year were Ben Scrivens, Joey Crabb, Ryan Hamilton, Nazem Kadri, Colton Orr, Matt Frattin, Joe Colborne, Carter Ashton, Mark Fraser, Korbinian Holzer, Jerry D'Amigo, and Jake Gardiner—all of whom moved up to play for the Maple Leafs at some point. Coach Dallas Eakins went on to be named the head coach of the Edmonton Oilers in 2013.

At the end of the 2017–18 season, the AHL Marlies won the Calder Cup and a number of players graduated to the big club including Andreas Johnsson, Justin Holl, Frederik Gauthier, Marin Marincin, Dmitri Timashov, Calle Rosen, Trevor Moore, Timothy Liljegren, Travis Dermott, Kasperi Kapanen, Pierre Engvall, and Garrett Sparks. As well, the winning coach of that championship, Sheldon Keefe, became coach of the parent Leafs.

The St. John's Maple Leafs and the Toronto Marlies are proof that a good farm system can be extremely valuable to the Toronto Maple Leafs.

83 Doug Gilmour

Toronto Maple Leaf fans were thrilled when centre Doug Gilmour joined the team in a trade with the Calgary Flames on January 2, 1992. Gilmour had a tremendous and immediate impact on the Leafs and nearly got the team into the '92 playoffs but fell just short. The following season was a different story as Gilmour posted the best season in Maple Leafs history when he recorded 127 points (32G, 95A) and the team was back in the postseason. While all Leaf fans showered Gilmour with deserved adoration, the gutsy pivot

Doug Gilmour is in the Hall of Fame. (Dennis Miles)

realized what it meant to Toronto fans to be back in contention and for the city to have a team they could be proud of once again.

On the night of April 13, 1993, the Leafs hosted the St. Louis Blues during the last home game of the regular season (which turned out to be a 2–1 overtime win for the Leafs). Prior to the start of the game Gilmour was recognized for his on-ice play (with former Leaf captain Darryl Sittler handing Gilmour a bronzed stick for breaking the club record for most points in one year—a mark held by Sittler) as well as off-ice work in the community (with Gilmour holding a youngster in his arms). Gilmour then took the microphone briefly to give out some acknowledgments of his own and said to the Maple Leaf Gardens crowd, "And last but not least, thanks Toronto fans. We're going to do something for you guys yet." A simple gesture from a great player but one not lost on the fans who appreciated the effort Gilmour gave to the team every night.

Once the '93 postseason began, Gilmour was the most out-standing player in the playoffs. His work in the first round helped to eliminate Detroit in seven games (including a four-point night in the last contest versus the Red Wings). He scored one of the most memorable overtime winning goals in Leafs history and got Toronto off to a good start against the St. Louis Blues in the next round while a three-point third period got the Leafs the opening night win versus Los Angeles in the Western Conference final in the third round. These are just a few of his most notable games in the playoffs. His on-ice leadership as a one-time Stanley Cup winner (with Calgary in 1989) was noticeable every shift on the ice.

Gilmour finished with 35 points (10G, 25A) in 21 playoff games played and if the Leafs had beaten the Kings in the Conference final, there can be little doubt he would have won the Conn Smythe Trophy (with all due respect to Montreal netminder Patrick Roy). It is also important to remember that the Leafs did not really have another centre to take the pressure off Gilmour's shoulders (John Cullen, Peter Zezel, Mike Eastwood, and Mike Krushelnyski all contributed to the Leafs playoff run but none could come close to Gilmour's production level) meaning he was being checked closely every single game.

Leafs general manager Cliff Fletcher called Gilmour "Mr. Hockey here in Toronto" while *Hockey Night in Canada* commentator Don Cherry said the Kingston, Ontario, native was, "the best player in the world today." Not many Maple Leaf players (if ever) have been called that but it was hard to argue against him at the time. It was even better to see a player live up to his word and give the Leaf fans a memory they will always cherish.

Gilmour was nearly as good in the 1994 playoffs although a leg injury sustained in the opening round against Chicago was hindering his play. Still, he managed 28 points in 18 games but a Western Conference final loss to Vancouver kept the Leafs from reaching the Stanley Cup final one more time. Gilmour was gone by February of 1997 in a deal with the New Jersey Devils but his play as a Maple Leaf was never forgotten. Leaf fans were hoping to recapture some magic in 2003 when he rejoined the Toronto team just before the playoffs, but an injury put an end to that dream after just one game back in a Toronto uniform.

84 Referee Kerry Fraser and the Maple Leafs

Maple Leaf fans will never forget the night of May 27, 1993, because a chance to go to the Stanley Cup final was possibly stolen from them because of a referee's call—or non-call, depending on your point of view. To set the scene for those who might not have seen it, the Maple Leafs tied the sixth game of the Western

Conference final in Los Angeles 4–4 on a late goal by captain Wendel Clark with his third of the night. The game headed for overtime and a goal for Toronto would put the team in the Stanley Cup final for the first time since 1967. However, just before the end of regulation time, winger Glenn Anderson was whistled off for charging by referee Kerry Fraser. It was one of many poor calls Fraser made throughout the night against the Maple Leafs but the man with the orange armband bought "the act" of Kings defenseman Rob Blake who sold the call.

Early in overtime, the Leafs had nearly killed the penalty off but were still on their end of the ice defending when Wayne Gretzky of the Kings accidently clipped Toronto's Doug Gilmour under the chin. The Leafs star smartly went down stopping the play and when he got up, he showed Fraser he was bleeding. The television replay clearly showed Gretzky trying to take the puck from Gilmour but his stick came up too high and cut the Leaf player. The three officials conferred but the decision was no penalty to Gretzky because nobody—including Fraser—actually saw Gretzky's stick do the damage. The still frames from the television broadcast clearly show Fraser looking right at the play with no obstruction in the way. Nevertheless, the face-off stayed in the Leafs end and Gretzky potted the overtime winner when he should have been in the penalty box. The goal tied the series at three games each and the Kings eked out a 5–4 win two nights later in Toronto to kill the Leafs' dream that year.

Fraser never appeared to be a referee who cut the Leafs any slack and to perhaps understand the reason why requires a flashback to October 16, 1985, during a game between Toronto and Washington. With an estimated 5,000 people in attendance (Toronto's attention was on the baseball Blue Jays who were playing Game 7 against the Kansas City Royals that same night), the Maple Leafs were up 5–4 on the Capitals mostly on the strength of a hat trick by captain Rick Vaive. In the final minute of play the Caps

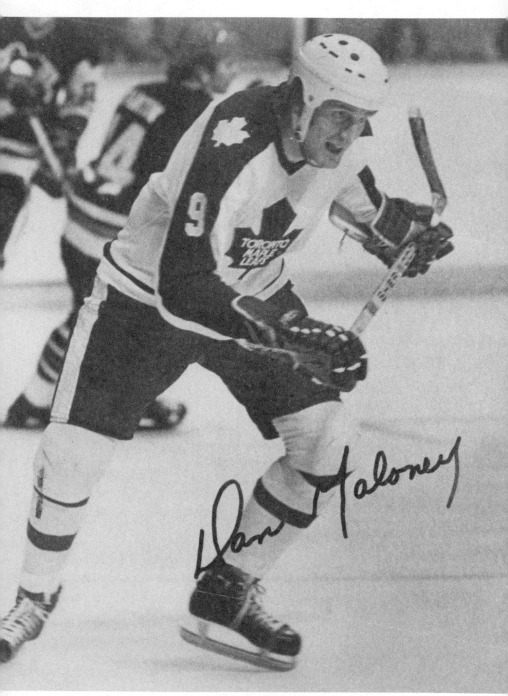

Dan Maloney was acquired in a trade with Detroit. (Robert Shaw)

pulled their goalie but Greg Terrion of the Leafs stripped the puck from Washington defenseman Larry Murphy and scored into the empty net for a 6–4 lead.

Not so fast said referee Fraser who pointed Terrion to the penalty box for tripping. Instead of being rewarded for his hard work Terrion was unfairly called for an infraction because Murphy simply turned the wrong way and fell. Mike Gartner tied it up with four seconds to play and the Capitals scored early in the overtime for the win.

Needless to say, Maple Leaf coach Dan Maloney was livid and stepped out on the ice after the game screaming at Fraser, and apparently chasing the referee down the lobby at Maple Leaf Gardens. "We had two points in the bag, we played a helluva game against one of the best teams in the league and what do we get for it? We get robbed," Maloney accurately summarized and it might have been nice to see the large Leaf bench boss (6'2", 195 pounds) actually get his hands on the much smaller (5'7") referee but it did not happen. It is a stretch to suggest that something that took place in 1985 affected another event that took place in 1993 but stranger things have happened. Whatever the case, the game versus Washington in October of 1985 was the first time Toronto fans had a strong dislike for Fraser, but it would certainly not be the last.

Fraser was also the referee who gave the Pittsburgh Penguins a goal during the 1999 playoffs that apparently he only saw—all the camera angles could not find the puck over the redline—and he denied a Maple Leaf goal during a game against the Islanders that cost Toronto a point and eventually a playoff spot during the 2006–07 season. It is pretty clear Fraser was never inclined to give the Leafs any sort of break and his retirement (after more than 1,900 regular season regular games and 260 playoff contests) in 2010 brought cheers from all fans of the Maple Leafs who will never forget the infamous night in Los Angeles!

85 The Fab Five: Maple Leaf Defensemen in 1992–93

When Toronto fans look back with fondness to the 1992–93 season of the Maple Leafs they often think of star forwards like Doug Gilmour and Wendel Clark, plus the exciting netminding of Felix Potvin or the fiery leadership behind the bench from coach Pat Burns. While all these names provided memorable performances in the regular season and playoffs, it was the Maple Leaf defensemen who were the backbone of the team. Featuring a nice mix of offence and defense, the largely veteran group provided the team with the necessary skills and experience to make the Leafs a serious contender.

Dave Ellett had the most natural talent and recorded 40 points during the regular season despite missing 14 games due to injury. The smooth skating Ellett added 12 more points in the postseason and proved that he still had plenty to give at the age of 28. Todd Gill recorded his best year playing alongside Ellett for most of the '92–'93 season and was the only Leaf blueliner to record double-digit goals (11). Veteran Jamie Macoun (acquired in the Gilmour deal with Calgary) gave the Leafs a physical presence at the age of 31. He also chipped in with 19 points. Macoun's experience teamed nicely with Sylvain Lefebvre who was picked up from Montreal for a third-round draft choice. Lefebvre was steady as a rock on the back end as was Bob Rouse who had 14 points in the regular season and then added another 11 in the playoffs. When the Leafs struggled out of the gate in the '93 playoffs, coach Burns felt most confident playing these five defensemen who helped right the ship and got the Leafs into the third round of the postseason. They were as good a group of five as there was in the entire NHL

Defenseman Dave Ellett (Dennis Miles)

that year but they wore down a little as the playoffs saw the Leafs play 21 games in 42 nights!

Dmitri Mironov (31 points in the regular season), Drake Berehowsky (19 points), Darryl Shannon, and Bob McGill also played defense for the Maple Leafs in '92–'93, but only Mironov saw any playoff action and the Russian was unprepared for the rigors of playoff hockey in North America. Berehowsky (only 21 at the time) and McGill were both injured and unavailable for the playoffs while Shannon did not have the confidence of his coach to dress him for any important game.

As a result, the Leafs went as far in the playoffs as the group who became known as the "Fab Five" could take them. Their collective performance nearly got the team to the final for the first time since 1967. This should not come as a surprise to any longtime fan of the Maple Leafs who knows that the team has always done well when they have blueliners who can play. In the 1930s the Leafs had Hap Day, King Clancy, and Red Horner patrolling along the blueline. When the team won four Stanley Cups in five years between 1947 and 1951, it was the likes of Jim Thomson, Gus Mortson, Bill Barilko, Garth Boesch, Wally Stanowski, Fern Flaman, and Bill Juzda. In winning three straight championships in the 1960s, Carl Brewer, Bob Baun, Allan Stanley, and Tim Horton were the best group of four defenders in the NHL. They were backed up by the likes of Kent Douglas, Al Arbour and Larry Hillman and later veteran Marcel Pronovost who was picked up in a deal with Detroit. It is noteworthy to mention that Lefebvre, Rouse, and Macoun all went on to win the Stanley Cup after they left the Maple Leafs.

If the Leafs are to win another championship, they will need to employ a group of defensemen who rival those of the glorious past.

86 Wendel Clark

When the Maple Leafs drafted Wendel Clark first overall in 1985, there were great expectations for the native of Kelvington, Saskatchewan. Converted to a left winger after a junior career that saw him shine as a defenseman for the Saskatoon Blades, Clark's first two seasons in Toronto were nothing short of sensational. He took the city by storm and scored 34 times as a rookie. He scored 37 the next season and his "rock 'em, sock 'em" style made Clark a major fan favourite. He would take on anybody and while he did not win all his fights, Clark won more than his share despite standing 5'11" and weighing in at 194 pounds. The Leafs it seemed had found a new leader for the next number of years but it took a turn for the worse in his third year when injuries piled up one on top of the other. A lower back injury kept nagging the truculent winger and it was a situation that was not dealt with properly when he played junior hockey.

Over the next three seasons with the Leafs Clark never appeared in more than 38 games and did not hit the 20-goal plateau even when he got into 63 games in 1990–91. Still he was named team captain in 1991 and that seemed to give Clark a bit of rejuvenation and he got into 66 games for the team in 1992–93. Pat Burns had taken over as coach and there was another star player on the team in the form of Doug Gilmour. Clark scored 17 times and was going to be looked upon as a key player in the '93 playoffs. However, the postseason did not start out well for Clark and he came under heavy fire from the media.

The Leafs lost the opening two games of the first-round series to the Detroit Red Wings by scores of 6–3 and 6–2. After the second defeat in Detroit many of the local scribes set their sights

Maple Leaf captain Wendel Clark (Dennis Miles)

on the Toronto captain more or less insinuating that he had done and shown little. One of the most vicious assaults said that Clark had been "the prettiest boy on the ice." The same writer went on to say, "He has been fading…fading…fading" and that if he has any bruising it must be "physiological." If that wasn't enough, Detroit tough guy Bob Probert was taunting the Leaf leader with his thoughts about how "Wendy" was not showing up for this series. How one person can be so responsible for a couple of bad losses is inexplicable but Clark would not take the bait. Instead he said the team would be better back home. He could have gotten angry and explained some simple facts (such as reminding everyone that the Leafs had not played at home yet) to the hockey writers of the day but he chose to be stoic and would let his playing be his ultimate response. Back at Maple Leaf Gardens the Leafs responded with a 4–2 win led by Clark's two-point (1G, 1A) night. The Leafs tied the series and then took the lead in the fifth game when Clark out fought Nicklas Lidstrom for a puck that he managed to get over to Mike Foligno for an overtime winning goal. Then Leafs won a thrilling Game 7 in Detroit in overtime to advance. Clark was instrumental in setting up the tying goal by Gilmour with an assist late in regulation, and then dug the puck out for a point shot that was redirected home by Nikolai Borschevsky for the winner.

There was no gloating by Clark who had taken all the criticisms in stride and he stayed hot for the next two rounds, getting the Leafs past St. Louis and almost by the Los Angeles Kings. Clark did it all versus the Kings by staging a memorable fight against Marty McSorley and then scoring five goals (including a hat trick in the sixth game) over the last two games of the series. It wasn't quite enough to get the Leafs through but Toronto fans would never forget the leadership shown by Clark even when everyone else told them to doubt the man wearing the "C" on his broad shoulder.

87 Nikolai Borschevsky

The Maple Leafs were looking for some scoring punch on the wing going into the 1992–93 season and decided to give a smallish (5'9", 180 pounds) Russian a chance to fill the need. Nikolai Borschevsky was drafted by 77ᵗʰ overall by Toronto in the '92 Entry Draft after he had performed well for Spartak Moscow (39 points in 40 games played) in 1991–92. The Leafs decided to risk the draft choice on a 27-year-old player who had never played in North America. He represented Russia at the Olympic Games in '92 (recording nine points—seven of them were goals—in eight games played) as well as the World Hockey Championships that same year. The move the Leafs made to bring Borschevsky over to Canada would pay off handsomely during the regular season and playoffs.

Despite his small stature Borschevsky displayed a willingness to mix it up all over the rink and to get to the front of the net where he showed some very nice hands. His 34 goals matched the most of any first-year player in Leaf history at the time Wendel Clark also shared the mark) while recording four game winners and 12 power-play markers. He finished the year with 74 points, good enough for second place in Leaf scoring during a magical season for the team.

The Leafs drew Detroit as their first-round opponent and the Norris Division winning Red Wings pounded on Toronto in the first two games of the series with 6–3 and 6–2 romps. In the second game Borschevsky was taken hard into the boards and suffered a serious cut under one eye. He was ruled out of the next five games but was able to dress for the seventh and deciding game in Detroit on May 1, 1993. It was an epic playoff contest that would need to be decided in overtime after the team completed sixty minutes tied 3–3. Early in the extra session Doug Gilmour took the puck in the

Nikolai Borschevsky scored the overtime winning goal versus Detroit in 1993.
(Dennis Miles)

Detroit end and slid it over to defenseman Bob Rouse at the point. Rouse let a drive go that was likely going to be stopped but there was Borschevsky right in front of the net to re-direct the puck past Red Wing netminder Tim Cheveldae for the series winner. The little Russian was mobbed by his ecstatic teammates and in a post-game interview with Ron MacLean *of Hockey Night in Canada* all Borschevsky could muster in English was the word "unbelievable."

Borschevsky ended up with nine points in 16 playoff games in the '93 postseason, concluding the height of his performance as a Maple Leaf. The following season saw the winger play in just 45 regular season games in 1993–94 (although he did record 34 points) but was able to only contribute four points in 15 postseason games. Borschevsky was badly hurt when he was crushed into the boards one game against the Florida Panthers and had to have his spleen removed. He was never quite the same and was soon given away to the Calgary Flames for a sixth-round draft choice. He also played briefly for the Dallas Stars before his 162-game NHL career came to close.

Borschevsky may have had one brief shining moment as a Maple Leaf but Toronto fans will always have good memories of the feisty Russian for his goal on "May Day" of 1993. The Toronto franchise had finally gained some respect back after many years of faltering and the winning goal versus Detroit helped boost the Leafs to within one game of the Stanley Cup final in 1993.

88 Dave Keon and Wayne Gretzky

Dave Keon and Wayne Gretzky are two Hall of Fame players who were highly skilled and had a deserved reputation for coming up big in crucial moments. The seventh game of a playoff series is the best time to shine as a clutch hockey player and both Keon and Gretzky certainly achieved great fame when they each scored a hat trick as they led their visiting teams to triumph. In fact, they are the only two players to accomplish the feat of scoring three goals on the road in a game that decided a postseason series.

Keon's great moment came on April 9, 1964 when the Leafs came into Montreal to close out the semi-final series between Montreal and Toronto. The Leafs had tied the series with a 3–0 win over Montreal at Maple Leaf Gardens two days earlier, but the hometown Habs were still favoured to win the final game. The Leafs (hoping to get to the Stanley Cup final to secure their third straight championship) had other ideas and Keon opened the scoring after the Leafs had hemmed the Habs in their own end. "The little man from Noranda made no mistake," said *Hockey Night in Canada* play-by-play broadcaster Danny Gallivan to a national audience on a Thursday evening.

Keon was just getting started. He scored a short-handed goal later in the first period when he took a pass from George Armstrong and sped away from the Montreal defenders to slap a shot past Montreal netminder Charlie Hodge. The Leafs held tight defensively after giving up a goal in the final frame but Keon closed off any hope for the Habs with just 11 seconds to play by scoring into the empty Montreal net for a 3–1 final. "A big night for a truly great player," Gallivan said after Keon's third tally. The slick Leaf centre had not done much on the scoreboard against Montreal

Dave Keon scored three goals in Game 7 versus Montreal in 1964.
(Harold Barkley Archives)

until the last game of the memorable series. He then helped the Leafs beat Detroit in the '64 final that also went seven games by scoring four times in the series including a key goal in the final contest at Maple Leaf Gardens.

Gretzky's great moment came against the Maple Leafs at the Gardens on May 29, 1993. The Los Angeles captain had scored a controversial overtime winning goal (he should have been in the penalty box for high sticking) in the sixth game of the series to force a seventh game. Gretzky opened the scoring on a short-handed effort to put the Leafs behind 1–0. Toronto battled back to even the score 2–2 in the second but the Gretzky blasted a shot past Leafs netminder Felix Potvin to give the Kings the lead once again. It was a crushing goal against the Leaf team that had battled so hard just to even the score.

The Leafs tied the game once more when Toronto captain Wendel Clark scored but the Kings got a late goal to go up 4–3. Gretzky then stuck the dagger in the heart of all Leafs fans when he circled the Toronto net and threw the puck out in front. The disk hit Leafs defenseman Dave Ellett on the leg and past Potvin. Ellett scored to make it 5–4 but the Leafs could not come up with the equalizer despite a frenzied assault on the Kings goal. Gretzky's final tally would prove to be the winner and the Kings would make it to the Stanley Cup final for the first time in their history (even though they would lose to Montreal in five games). Gretzky would say his performance at the Gardens was his best ever NHL game over his illustrious career that featured many highlights. Leaf fans could never disagree with that assessment.

Scoring three goals in any playoff game is not an easy feat by any means but to do so on the road is even more of a great accomplishment considering there is a packed arena screaming and cheering against everything you are trying to do. It took great players like Keon and Gretzky to accomplish what might seem to be impossible and they are still the only two players in NHL history to finish a series in such fashion—a very fitting tribute to both stars.

89 The Mighty Pat Quinn

By the late 1960s the Toronto Maple Leaf defense was being entirely rebuilt with Tim Horton as the only holdover from the four Stanley Cup years in the same decade. Blueliners like Jim McKenny, Brian Glennie, Rick Ley, Jim Dorey, and Mike Pelyk were going to form the nucleus of Toronto's defensive corps. One other name that was on that list for a brief time was a hulk-like (6'3", 215 pounds) defenseman named Pat Quinn, a native of Hamilton Ontario. Quinn was in the Detroit organization as a junior but the Maple Leafs picked him up from St. Louis in a cash deal in March of 1968 (a transaction that completed a 1967 deal which saw the Maple Leafs send the rights to Dickie Moore to St. Louis).

The 25-year-old Quinn was assigned to the Tulsa Oilers of the Central Hockey League for the 1967–68 season by the Leafs. Quinn could play the game but his large size held back his skating somewhat. He sported a flowing black mane which made him look even more imposing to the opposition. One of Quinn's teammates on the Oilers for part of that year was Pelyk who was just out of junior hockey. Pelyk tells a very interesting story about his teammate:

"We were playing Fort Worth one game and they were a pretty good team. The Oilers had a group of young, aggressive guys who were just learning the pro game. During the game I decided for no particular reason that I was going to hit the Fort Worth tough guy Lou Marcon (he had played in the NHL a little bit with the Detroit Red Wings in the late 1950s). Marcon was short and stocky (5'9", 168 pounds) with hair flying everywhere and a reputation for being aggressive (at least in the minors). I got a chance to line Marcon up for a hit and I let him have it pretty good. Everyone thought I had lost my mind hitting their toughest player but I just didn't care. But I knew I had to watch myself the rest of the game because Marcon was sure to come after me. Pat Quinn told me not to worry—he had my back.

Leaf defenseman Pat Quinn gets his stick up against Bobby Orr of Boston.
(York University Archives/ *Toronto Telegram* Collection)

Sure enough, the puck got dumped into the corner on my side and I had to turn back to get it. Marcon was on the ice and he starts making a beeline right for me to give me my payback. Quinn was out with me and he saw what was about to happen and met up with Marcon before the Fort Worth winger ever got near me. Bam! One shot and Marcon was down. Pat just plowed him with one punch. The whole arena was stunned and the Fort Worth bench could not believe what they had just seen. No one dared to challenge Pat and we went on to win the game something like 6–2. After Pat's knockdown of Marcon we owned them and the Oilers eventually beat Fort Worth in the CHL finals to win the championship."

Quinn was much the same protective teammate when he joined the Leafs for 40 games in 1968–69 and began a rather celebrated feud with Boston superstar Bobby Orr. The Bruins defenseman gave up quite a bit of size to Quinn but he never backed away from the Leafs tough guy. During the '69 playoffs, Quinn knocked Orr out with a flying body check that featured a good amount of elbow to Orr's head. Orr was carrying the puck with his head down just as he was approaching the Boston blueline to clear the zone when Quinn lowered the boom. The Boston Garden crowd was ready to lynch Quinn for his assault on their golden boy and tried to get at him while he sat in the penalty box. The other Leaf players came off the bench to rescue Quinn and he somehow got out of Boston with his life but he never backed away from anyone.

Quinn was with the Leafs for one more year in 1969–70 before he went to Vancouver and then Atlanta to finish out a 606-game NHL career. He would come back to Toronto in 1998 to coach the Leafs for seven seasons, taking the team to the Eastern Conference final twice while missing the playoffs just once. Quinn also coached Canada to a gold medal at the 2002 Winter Olympic Games.

90 The New Maple Leaf Gardens and Coca-Cola Coliseum

When Maple Leaf Gardens hosted its final hockey game in 1999, nobody was quite sure what was going to happen to the historic building which first opened on November 12, 1931. The building on the corner of Carlton and Church Streets in Toronto had been home to the Maple Leafs for 68 years but the main tenant was gone for good and other important events (like major concerts and a variety of other sports) would also be directed to the Air Canada Centre. The Gardens had been declared a National Historic Site of Canada in 2007 and a statement released at the time of the declaration:

> ...Maple Leaf Gardens is one of the most renowned "shrines" in the history of hockey... the largest arena in the country when it was built, it was one of the country's foremost venues for large-scale sporting events such as boxing matches and track meets, and non-sporting events such as concerts, rallies and political gatherings, religious services and opera... the Gardens holds a special place in the country's popular culture: here Canadians welcomed a wide range of cultural icons from The Beatles to the Metropolitan Opera, to Team Canada vs. the Soviets, from Winston Churchill to the Muhammad Ali-George Chuvalo fight.

The Maple Leafs did not have an obvious plan for the old building but they were not about to give up control to anyone who might use the historic venue as a way to compete with their new home. Proposals came and went without much action but eventually two organizations stepped forward and made a deal with Maple Leaf Sports and Entertainment to restructure the Gardens entirely. Loblaws' food store took over a large part of the building (some 70,000 square feet) to create a massive grocery story while Ryerson University took over most of the rest of the structure which included creating a full-sized hockey rink on the third floor which can seat between 2,500 and 2,700 spectators. Student athletic facilities take up the rest of the space but the outside of the building still has "Maple Leaf Gardens" on the marquee.

While it is good to see that the Gardens retains something of its glorious past with the Ryerson Rams becoming the main hockey tenant, it would have been better to see the arena integrity kept in place just like when the Maple Leafs played there. The only parts that are still intact are the walls and the roof—otherwise nobody would recognize it as the once treasured home of the Maple Leafs. Keeping centre ice intact should have been a priority with 5,000 to 7,500 seats to be kept as a functioning arena. There was no support for such an idea (especially after the Marlies were slotted into the Ricoh Coliseum) and thus the Gardens remains just a shadow of what it once was and what it meant to Toronto. Still, it is worth a visit for those who live here and for those who come to Toronto and want to see part of the city's great heritage.

The other place to see would be the Ricoh Coliseum now Coca Cola Coliseum which is the home to the Maple Leafs main farm team, the Toronto Marlies of the American Hockey League. Renovated at a cost of about $38 million in 2003, the Coliseum first had the Edmonton Oilers farm team (the Toronto Roadrunners) as its main tenant but that lasted all of one season. The Leafs decided to bring their top minor league affiliate club to the grounds of the Canadian National Exhibition (not very far from the Air Canada Centre) and moved into the 9,700-seat capacity Ricoh in 2005. They have enjoyed some success there including a Calder Cup championship in 2018 under current Leaf coach Sheldon Keefe.

The Coliseum is not the prettiest of places to see a game and has in fact been called dark and dungy by more than one observer. This may be part of the reason why regular season attendance is not as high as hoped and the Leafs had to restructure their pricing and not schedule many games on Saturday nights. The Marlies play a very gritty style of play at home and the fans do come out to support the team at playoff time. time.

91 Toronto Maple Leafs Fan Talks

Leaf Nation is fortunate to have opportunities to discuss the ups and downs of their team with other fans and learn about the past from various alumni.

There have been fans clubs in the past, from "Bud's Club" in the 1940s to the "Toronto Maple Leaf Booster Club" in the 1990s. Today, there is the "Club Maple Leafs" for the youngest members of Leaf Nation.

The "Toronto Maple Leafs Official Fan Club Public Group" on Facebook keeps fans informed daily. There are many other online groups dedicated to the Leafs as well.

There are also group events where alumni appear as guests and video tributes are shown.

One of the longest running get-togethers is the monthly "Original 6 Alumni Lunch" that had its start in the 1970s with former Leafs from the '40s to the '60s. Some of the regulars included Harry Watson, Cal Gardner, Sid Smith, Tod Sloan, Danny Lewicki, John McCormack, and Wally Stanowski, among others. The "Whirling Dervish" Stanowski was a regular until past the age of 95, still telling stories about the Leafs 1942 comeback win. Sadly, most of the originals have passed on, but organizer Al Shaw and former players Ron Hurst, Pete Conacher, Bob Nevin, Dick Duff, Bob Baun, and others have kept the tradition going.

The format has changed over the years, with various hockey personalities welcome. The crowd can now view video tributes to alumni guests and all the sessions are captured by professional photographer Lora Evans and shared on social media to a huge following. A new feature is a Q&A session with a former player, conducted by Scott Morrison.

The lunch group also welcomes family members of the former players. Included are the Primeau, Smith, Stanowski, Lewicki, and Bower relations.

Another group session that has been popular with Leaf fans is the "Inside the Room" Nights hosted by Mike Wilson at his Leaf museum. Each night had a different theme highlighting a topic from past and present Toronto players or teams.

A new monthly event promises to be very exciting for Leaf fans. "Toronto Talks Hockey" will be held at the Mattamy Centre, better known to us as "Maple Leaf Gardens," which is an appropriate venue for Leaf talk. The event will be hosted by hockey historians Kevin Shea, Todd Denault, and Paul Patskou. The first session will focus on Toronto's famous "Kid Line" of the 1930s, with relatives of Joe Primeau, Harvey "Busher" Jackson, and Charlie Conacher present.

At these events, its not uncommon for the talk to shift to the present-day Leafs, in particular the thoughts of the former players. That's when it gets really interesting.

92 Ken Dryden

When the Maple Leafs hired goaltending legend Ken Dryden to run the team as president in 1997, they were certainly thinking outside the box. The multi-talented, intellectual Dryden was not even in hockey at the time but it was believed that with his winning background as a player with the Montreal Canadiens (sharing in six Stanley Cups triumphs with the mighty Habs) and with his way of approaching old problems with new and innovative solutions, that he could lead the Maple Leafs to new heights. Except for his first season with the team, the Maple Leafs did very well under Dryden and were always a competitive team going to the conference final on two occasions (1999 and 2002).

One of Dryden's new ideas was to get Maple Leaf fans to tell their stories about their love of the team with photos and anecdotes. The best stories were chosen to be put on season tickets for the 2000–01 season and it was one of the best ideas the team has ever come up with to connect with their fans. There were no shortage of submissions and the hard part was picking the ones that would appear on the tickets for each and every home game.

One of the very best came from longtime season ticket holder Tom Gaston, who wrote that he was so proud to be chosen to represent all Leaf fans during the multi-car parade from Maple Leaf Gardens to the Air Canada Centre when the old building closed and the new one opened in February of 1999. Gaston was proud that the car he was riding in had a sign that said, "Superfan Tom Gaston." Before he passed away Gaston had a book published with his memories of the Maple Leafs including many special moments from the Gardens. Gaston's photo and story appear on the Saturday, October 7, 2000 tickets for the Toronto-Montreal game, a contest the Leafs won 2–0.

Another heart-warming story and photo came from Bruce Brigham of Barrie, Ontario on the Wednesday, November 15, 2000 tickets for the Leafs-Flyers game that night. The colour photo shows Brigham's two boys (Mark and Dean) decked out in Leaf sweaters circa 1969 and the story says Bruce was a 25-year subscriber to the Gardens and that his love of players like Ted Kennedy, Dave Keon, and Red Kelly made the Brigham family lifelong supporters of the blue and white.

Joe and Cathryn Doucher sent a photo of them getting married in Vancouver in 1996 in their Maple Leaf sweaters! Joe recalled his favourite moment being when Lanny McDonald scored the overtime winner to beat the New York Islanders in the 1978 playoffs. The Douchers' story and photo appeared on a ticket set for Home Game 2, Round 2 of the 2001 playoffs, which was played on May 3, 2001 at the ACC with the Leafs winning 3–1. The Leafs would ultimately lose that series in seven games to the New Jersey Devils.

The Primeau family has had season's tickets to Leaf games since 'Gentleman' Joe Primeau with the help of Conn Smythe personally picked 8 seats in the original Maple Leaf Gardens in 1931. In fact, Joe Primeau may have been the first ever Leafs season ticket subscriber. Not only have the Primeau's kept their close relationship with the Leafs by retaining their seats but Suzanne Primeau, the granddaughter of Joe was asked to help cut the ribbon with then President Ken Dryden and the VP of Imperial Oil at the opening of the "Esso Memories and Dreams" room at the new Air Canada Centre. The Primeau's story appears on the February 3, 2004, game ticket.

More stories and photos were submitted over the next two seasons and they covered a wide spectrum of fans from the youngest to the oldest. Dryden's idea found a special niche that was perfect

An Original 6 game vs Chicago ticket exhibits the connection of the Primeau family with the Toronto Maple Leafs. Joe Primeau had taken the opening faceoff against the Hawks when Maple Leaf Gardens opened.
(Photo courtesy of Suzanne Primeau)

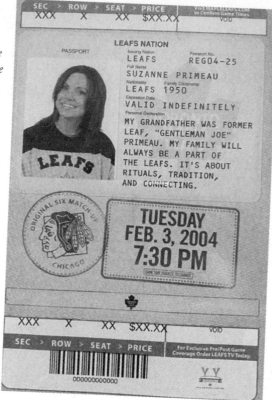

because it gave the fans some ownership of the Maple Leafs season tickets and it is the loyal season ticket holders who drive the love of the team more than any other group of fans.

As for Dryden, his other interests (writer, commentator, political ambitions) slowly but surely pulled him away from the Leafs. He also lost a power struggle (to Leafs coach and general manager Pat Quinn) when new ownership took over and he left the team in 2004 to run for Canadian Parliament as a member of the Liberal Party. He was elected on his first try.

93 Next Generation Game—Leafs Revive "Young Canada Night"

The "Next Generation" game at Scotiabank Arena was played on December 23, 2019, against the visiting Carolina Hurricanes. It was a special event with many youngsters in attendance. It's a tradition that was revived a few years ago based on "Young Canada Night," an event that began in December 1933 at Maple Leaf Gardens. Foster Hewitt's eight-year-old son, Bill, had called the play for part of the game on radio. In the 1960s, Bill's son Bruce did the same on the TV broadcasts.

Starting in the 1933–34 season, "Young Canada Night" was a longtime tradition on the Saturday night home game closest to Christmas. Originally called "Kiddies Christmas Special," on December 23, 1933, fans were encouraged to buy a ticket to see the Montreal Maroons play the Leafs and to bring a child of 15 years old or younger to the game. Season ticket holders would be provided with a "kid's" ticket at a special reduced price and eventually for free.

The next season the event was renamed "Young Canada Night." On December 22, 1934, the Stanley Cup champions Chicago Black Hawks with Howie Morenz were entertaining the young crowd.

At the time, Maple Leaf Gardens was only a few years old and the Leafs were looking for a marketing campaign to increase attendance. It was a brilliant idea to attract the next generation of fans using the Christmas season and gifts as bait.

On December 24, 1949, as usual young Bill Hewitt called the play at the start of the third period, but there was an extra treat for the radio listening audience. The usual between-periods radio intermission "Hot Stove League" was billed as "Junior Hot Stove" with the sons of famous hockey personalities taking over and discussing the game.

Usual "Hot Stove" host Wes McKnight had his son, Gregg McKnight, participating, along with Hap Day's son, Kerry; Lionel Conacher's son, Lionel Jr.; and D'Alton Coleman, son of sportswriter Jim Coleman.

The tradition continued into the 1960s, with Bruce Hewitt doing the television play by play under the watchful eye of proud

Max Keys began to play the piano at 5½ years old with some help from his mom. Nine months later he was playing the organ for the Toronto Maple Leafs alongside Jimmy Holmstrom. Jimmy helped Max transition to the organ and taught him the classic Maple Leafs organ jingles. Max plays everything by ear and memory. (Photo courtesy of Max's mom, Tea Cheney)

grandfather Foster, who called the opening game at Maple Leaf Gardens in 1931.

"Young Canada Night" was largely forgotten until recent years, when Maple Leafs Sports and Entertainment revived the tradition with a new name: "Next Generation Game" on the last home game before Christmas.

The latest edition of the "Next Generation Game" on December 23, 2019, with the Leafs hosting the Carolina Hurricanes, was a wild contest that the Leafs won 8–6 in a thrilling third-period comeback.

Maxim Keys, a six-year-old prodigy, played the organ, giving longtime organist Jimmy Holmstrom a break. Doug Gilmour's 11-year-old daughter Victoria was the "in-game" host.

Also attending the game were at least 30 Leaf Alumni with their grandkids in a special Alumni Box called "the Gondola."

After the game, Leaf coach Sheldon Keefe was asked about the "Next Generation" idea:

"I think the whole concept behind it is outstanding. I think if we didn't make a next generation of fans here today, I'm not sure we ever will, with everything that was at play. I thought it was great. The kids on the bench were cool, the interviews before the game, it's awesome and it's nice to be a part of that."

Kudos to the Leaf organization for reviving this "tradition."

94 Worst Free Agent Signings by the Maple Leafs Since 1980

1. **David Clarkson**—Based on term, dollars, and lack of production.
2. **Stephan Robidas**—Why sign a 37-year-old defenseman coming off a broken leg to a three-year contract? Disappeared after the first year.
3. **Jeff Finger**—Who signs a 29-year-old career minor league defenseman with only one NHL season under his belt to a four-year contract? Was this a case of mistaken identity? Could be. Leafs already had a surplus of right-handed defensemen.
4. **Rickard Wallin**—Did he come over to babysit goaltender Jonas Gustavsson, a fellow Swede? Scored two goals in 60 games.
5. **Anders Eriksson**—Stanley Cup–winning defenseman played well in Detroit but was mediocre as a Leaf. Former first rounder of Detroit played 38 games with Leafs, contributing two assists and suspect defense.
6. **Brett Lebda**—Played reasonably well as a Red Wing but then forgot how to play hockey altogether as a Maple Leaf.
7. **Robert Reichel**—Signed to a three-year contract and it was apparent early that he was not the same player after two years in Europe.
8. **Mike Craig**—He could score against the Leafs when he was with Dallas but did virtually nothing when he played for Toronto. And it cost them Peter Zezel and Grant Marshall.
9. **Jason Blake**—Who signs a 35-year-old to a five-year contract? John Ferguson Jr., that's who.
10. **Mike Komisarek**—Valuable defender in Montreal but could not find his game as a Maple Leaf.

95 Bryan McCabe

When the Maple Leafs acquired defenseman Bryan McCabe in a trade with the Chicago Blackhawks, it marked the fourth team for the still very young career of the 25-year-old. McCabe had been originally drafted by the New York Islanders in 1993 (40th overall) but was dealt to Vancouver along with Todd Bertuzzi in a deal that saw the Islanders receive Trevor Linden in return. McCabe left the New York club as team captain indicating he was seen as a team leader. He played two seasons in Vancouver but had to be included in a deal that saw the Canucks land the Sedin twins (Henrick and Daniel) in return with McCabe going to Chicago. McCabe was being moved but that brought an excellent return to the team he was leaving.

When Mike Smith took over as general manager of the Blackhawks, he continued his historically preferred acquisitions of mainly European-born players (especially Russians). The Leafs could not agree to terms on a new contract for Moscow born blue-liner Alexander Karpovtsev. The Leafs had received a good year out of Karpovtsev in 1998–99 but were not ready to make any sort of long-term deal at big bucks. Smith jumped at the opportunity to acquire Karpovtsev and the Toronto club happily ended up with the St. Catharines-born defenseman McCabe on their team. It was one of Leafs general manager Pat Quinn's better trades.

McCabe seemed to finally find a home as a Maple Leaf and when he was paired with fellow blueliner Tomas Kaberle, the two found a chemistry that served them both very well. In seven seasons with the Maple Leafs McCabe recorded 297 points (83G, 214A) in 523 games played. His best offensive totals came in 2005–06 when he scored 19 goals (fourth highest total for a Leaf defenseman in

Toronto defenseman Bryan McCabe (#24) (Dennis Miles)

one season) and added 49 assists for 68 points (the third highest one season total for a Toronto blueliner). He also played for Team Canada at the 2006 Winter Olympics. Those achievements went along with a second team all-star berth for his play in 2003–04—the first Toronto defenseman to get an end of season all-star nomination since Borje Salming in 1980!

Naturally the Leafs had to reward the 6'2", 220-pound defense-man with a rich contract that included a "no movement" clause meaning he could not be traded, demoted or even placed on waivers. Kaberle also scored a new deal and it looked like the two would stay in Toronto for the rest of their careers. But when the team started to slide in the standings and McCabe began trying to justify his hefty salary, it all started to go downhill in quick fashion. Soon fans forgot about the great shot from the point on the power-play and began to boo McCabe at practically every turn. While it was certainly a fact that McCabe was not playing as he had before there was really no justification for booing a highly regarded defenseman.

Unlike other players who refused to be moved (invoking their no trade clauses), McCabe told interim Toronto general manager Cliff Fletcher to come to him if there was any trade on the table Leaf management wanted to make. He played out the 2007–08 season as a Leaf but accepted a deal to the Florida Panthers for the start of the following year. Rather than being a selfish player McCabe did what was best for him and the Maple Leafs who received a quality player in Mike Van Ryn when the deal was completed. McCabe should have been applauded for his mature response to a bad situation in Toronto but some would always recall his final days as a Leaf which were very hard to watch.

If Van Ryn had stayed healthy, Leaf fans would have been grateful to McCabe for allowing the deal but a couple of ugly hits ruined his career after just 27 games in Toronto. McCabe mean-while played in Florida for most of the next three seasons before closing out his career with a brief stay as a New York Ranger. He finished with 528 career points in 1,135 career games in the NHL—a career to be appreciated and not derided in any way.

96 Joe Nieuwendyk and Brian Leetch

The 2003–04 season had one of the more interesting teams in Toronto hockey history and in many ways modelled after the 1967 Stanley Cup champions by the end of the season.

The '03–'04 Maple Leafs set a club record with 103 points based on a 45–24–10–3 mark during the regular season (the three games at the end of the record is the number of times the Leafs lost in overtime that year—a season that did not have shootouts). This team made their mark starting on the night of November 22, 2003 when they defeated the Vancouver Canucks 5–3 to close off a six-game road trip. The Leafs won the next seven games in a row before St. Louis took a 3–2 decision at the Air Canada Centre in overtime. But the Leafs came back to win six of the next seven games and the only blemish over that stretch of games was a 2–2 tie in Washington against the Capitals. In total from November 22 to December 22, 2003, the Maple Leafs went 16 consecutive games without a regulation time loss (14–0–1–1) and only one of their victories was in overtime!

What made this team so good? The Leafs were loaded with great veterans like Mats Sundin (31 goals), Owen Nolan (48 points), Gary Roberts (28 goals), Alex Mogilny (30 points in 37 games played), Mikael Renberg (12 goals and 25 points), Ken Klee (29 points), Bryan Marchment (106 penalty minutes), and the ageless Ed Belfour (34 wins and 10 shutouts) in goal. Another key veteran acquisition was centre Joe Nieuwendyk who came to the Maple Leafs as a free agent. He scored 22 times and totaled 50 points in 64 games played and gave the team the strongest presence at the centre ice position in many years.

This Maple Leaf club had its share of younger players including Nik Antropov (31 points), Alexei Ponikarovsky (28 points), and Matt Stajan (27 points), while Darcy Tucker (21 goals), Bryan McCabe (53 points), and Tomas Kaberle (31 points) were still in their prime years. The Leafs also had good depth in the form of players such as Tom Fitzgerald, plus tough guys like Tie Domi, Nathan Perrott and Wade Belak.

In the hopes of securing their first trip to the final since '67, the Maple Leafs went out and added more veterans like centre Ron Francis and veteran rearguard Calle Johansson for the stretch drive. However, their biggest acquisition was all-star defenseman Brian Leetch from the New York Rangers. The Leafs gave up two prospects and a number one and number two draft choices (none of which came back to haunt the Leafs for a change) to the Rangers to land Leetch. The smooth skating rearguard played some great hockey for the Leafs (15 points in 15 games plus eight points in the playoffs) albeit for a short period of time.

The additions to the Leafs roster should have made the team more formidable but Toronto had to go seven games to eliminate the Ottawa Senators in the first round of the playoffs. Nieuwendyk was terrific in the seventh game scoring twice to lead his team to victory and ending Ottawa captain Daniel Alfredsson's boast that the Senators would beat the Toronto side—much to the delight of Toronto fans of course.

However, the Ottawa series took a lot out of older Leafs and they were ousted in six games by Philadelphia in the next round when Jeremy Roenick scored an overtime winner at the Air Canada Centre. A dream ending of a veteran team winning the Cup much like the Leafs did in '67 was suddenly vanquished. Both Leetch and Nieuwendyk were gone when the NHL resumed play after the lockout in the 2005–06 season. The Leafs did not return to the playoffs until 2013.

97 Best Opening Ceremony: Felix Potvin and Darcy Tucker

Pregame ceremonies have become standard fare right across the NHL. Most teams use the pregame starting time as a way to honour current or past players for some level of achievement. The ceremonies are usually brief in nature unless it involves the honouring of a player whose sweater is going to be raised to the rafters of the home arena. For a variety of reasons, the Maple Leafs have not been especially good at producing pregame presentations. Often it is because the presentation is too long with too much narrative coming from the public address microphone. Another problem is that the Leafs do too many pregame ceremonies and the fans get a little restless knowing the start of the game is going to be delayed once again.

The Leafs were not great at postgame ceremonies either. When Maple Leafs Gardens closed in February of 1999, the closing did not seem to have a beginning, a middle, and most certainly no ending of significance. There were some nice touches that night, like Canadian legend Anne Murray singing *The Maple Leaf Forever,* but that was about it for memorable moments notwithstanding the appearance of many great former players. Since that time the Leafs have certainly improved how they conduct pregame ceremonies and the postgame three star selection now features any Maple Leaf player named as game star giving out a stick to someone in the lower bowl of Scotiabank Arena.

The Leafs have had to endure their share of criticism for their presentations but on the night of January 21, 2013 the organization got it just right. The occasion was the start of the abbreviated 2012–13 season and many ex-Leafs were at the entry to welcome fans back to the NHL. Gary Leeman, Jim McKenny, Rob Pearson, and Dave Reid were some of the former Leafs signing autographs for fans as they entered the building. The 48th Highlanders military marching band was on the ice just as they had been when the Gardens opened in 1931. Another tradition that started at the Gardens was the ceremonial opening face-off and this time the Maple Leafs had something special in mind.

Astronaut Chris Hadfield, a noted Maple Leafs fan, was shown on the scoreboard from the international space station. "I am proud to be the first member of Leafs Nation to be in space," Hadfield told the cheering crowd. Then he "dropped" the puck from his location and it landed in the glove of goalie Felix Potvin. The former Leaf netminder then dropped the puck to Darcy Tucker who took an elevator to an awaiting Darryl Sittler the former Leaf captain. Sittler ran through the bowels and corridors of the ACC and right over to the Leaf bench where the legendary Johnny Bower took the puck to centre ice. All four former stars took part in the face-off between Leaf captain Dion Phaneuf and Buffalo captain Jason Pominville. The Leafs were edged 2–1 by the Sabres that night, but everyone loved the involvement of Hadfield and the Leaf legends for the opening draw.

Toronto fans are used to seeing Bower and Sittler around the building but Potvin and Tucker had not been so visible since their retirement. Potvin will always be remembered for his great performance in the 1993 playoffs which nearly saw the Leafs in the Stanley Cup final. Tucker will be fondly recalled for his all-out, feisty approach to the game and especially for his play in the 2002 playoffs when he played with an injury to his collarbone. It was good to see new faces added to the pregame ceremonies in Toronto which have seemed to take a turn for the better.

On February 8, 2014 the Leafs honoured the 1964 Stanley Cup champions at centre ice before the start of Toronto's game against Vancouver. The ceremony was direct, to the point, and each former player present was given a quick but significant statement about his contribution to the championship. The recognition for the '64 champs seemed to strike the right chord (even if the fans were a little subdued) and the current Leafs went on to beat the Canucks 3–1.

98 The Barilko Puck

Bill Barilko's overtime goal to win the Stanley Cup for the Leafs on April 21, 1951, is thought to be the most iconic goal in the history of the franchise. That would make the winning-goal puck historically important to be preserved and displayed for many fans to see. "Bashing Bill" went missing on a fishing trip that summer and the wreckage was only discovered shortly after the Leafs won their next Stanley Cup 11 years later. Many younger Leaf fans were familiar with the story because of the Tragically Hip song "50 Mission Cap." And if they wanted to see the actual puck, it is on display at the Hockey Hall of Fame in Toronto.

Or is it?

Back in the 1970s, a man named George Fletcher donated the Barilko puck to the HHOF. It was given to him by Jimmy Main, who was situated in the handicapped section behind the Montreal net in the front row. According to one account, a Montreal player shot the puck over the glass right after the winning goal by Barilko.

Another version had referee Bill Chadwick picking up the puck and handing it over to Main, who was seated in his wheelchair next to the goal judge, telling him to take it home to his mother. Whatever the story, the famous puck ended up on display at the HHOF.

However, in 2016, Dan Donahue from Hamilton, Ontario, notified the Hall that he had the winning goal puck from the 1951 Leaf Stanley Cup victory. The Donahue family's intent was to have the puck exhibited for the Toronto Maple Leafs centennial celebrations in 2017. But the HHOF claimed the famous puck was already on display.

The account of how the HHOF came in possession of the Barilko puck was well known, but what was the Donahue family's story? Dan explained that his dad, Harry, who was 16 at the time, had approached an usher by the boards and received permission to go on the ice to retrieve the puck, and the puck has been sitting on a mantle in the Donahue home ever since.

Standing (left to right): Mike Wilson, Dan Donahue (whose father retrieved the puck), Paul Patskou, David McNeil (his father, Gerry McNeil, was the Montreal goalie who was scored on), Craig Campbell (Hockey Hall of Fame resource manager), Jim Amodeo, and Kevin Shea (author of Barilko: Without a Trace*). Kneeling and holding the puck is Barry Klisanich and to the right of him is Paul Lewicki, whose dad played in the game with the Leafs.*

The obvious inclination would be to believe that the HHOF had the real Barilko puck and not an individual who 65 years later decided to reveal that his family had the puck.

But what evidence is there to confirm either claim? This is where things get interesting. The three photos from different angles of Bill Barilko flying through the air after scoring on Gerry McNeil offers no clues. There are newsreels, but the focus is on the goal and the celebration. Maybe a closer look at the newsreel footage might help. There is no television footage, as the Leafs did not start televising their games until November 1, 1952.

Fortunately, video archivist and hockey historian Paul Patskou recalled that the Toronto Maple Leafs had filmed their games since the mid-1940s for instructional purposes. He had in his possession the game film from April 21, 1951, but hadn't viewed it for years. Assuming the camera kept rolling, what are the chances that it would capture the referee handing the puck to Jimmy Main or the angry Hab player shooting the puck over the glass?

A closer look at the newsreel film revealed that the referee is seen quickly skating off the ice, making no attempt to retrieve the puck. Nor did any Montreal player shoot the puck into the crowd.

The game film shot by Shanty MacKenzie, the building manager at Maple Leaf Gardens, has never been shown publicly. Upon checking the game film, which included extensive postgame footage, it is apparent that as both teams were skating off the ice, there was a lone figure sliding his way down towards the Montreal net. It doesn't appear to be a photographer, newspaper reporter, or part of the MLG staff. Perhaps that was Harry Donahue! Could there be some merit to the Donahue family claim? According to Dan Donahue, the description fits his dad as a 16-year-old.

The newsreel film has already cast doubt regarding the validity of the story told to the HHOF.

Still to be determined was if the puck was still lying in the back of the net.

Dan Donahue takes up the investigation and discovers that the City of Toronto Archives had previously unseen photo images. And they clearly show that the puck is still in the net while the Leafs celebrate and the Canadiens are standing around in a confused state. And when the photo is enlarged, a grainy image appears of the octagonal shape of the crest on NHL pucks used in that era, which matches the Donohue Barilko puck. The HHOF Barilko puck has a circular and smaller Spalding crest, which was in use from 1920 to 1942 in the NHL. The Donohue's Barilko puck has an emblem that was used in NHL games from 1950 to 1958.

Together with the visual evidence presented and the type of puck used, it appears that the HHOF version of events should be called in to doubt, while the Donahue version becomes more plausible. The Donahue family is still hopeful of displaying the puck used to score possibly the most memorable goal in Toronto Maple Leaf history.

99 The Return of David Keon

One of the hot topic issues among fans in Leaf Nation was the "honouring" of sweaters and not retiring the numbers as other teams have. But it wasn't only the fans who were upset with the policy. So were the retired players, in particular Dave Keon, who had become estranged from the organization. To those who had seen Keon play, not only was he a fan favourite, but he was possibly the best Maple Leaf ever. The slick centreman left the Leafs for the World Hockey Association after the 1974–75 season on bad terms when he felt he was not wanted by then-Leafs owner Harold Ballard. When Keon desired to return to the NHL a few years later to join the New York Islanders, the Leafs demanded too much for his rights. He did return when the WHA merged with the NHL for the 1970–80 season, playing three more seasons with the Hartford Whalers retiring at age 42.

Over the years, Keon had made infrequent visits to Maple Leaf Gardens and the Air Canada Centre for tributes, such as honouring the championship teams of the 1960s. Keon attended because of the teammates he'd gone to war with and not necessarily for the Leaf organization.

It was thought that Keon was keeping his distance from the Leafs because of his dislike for Harold Ballard, but the ornery former Leaf owner had long since passed. Keon himself would not elaborate on exactly why he wasn't part of the Leaf family.

When "Legends Row" was first announced, Dave Keon would have been one of the first to be considered for a statue. But no sense having an unveiling if the player refuses to accept the honour.

Many fans wondered why his No. 14 wasn't lifted to the rafters like other famous numbers, such as No. 27 for Frank Mahovlich and Darryl Sittler. But it bothered David to see his sweater number being used by other (lesser) players; he saw it as an insult. Leaf fans were insulted too when the likes of John Kordic wore the famed No. 27.

Previous Leaf management types tried to convince the four-time Stanley Cup winner to return to the fold but were unsuccessful. However, on January 21, 2016, Leaf president Brendan Shanahan announced, "There have been hundreds of great players who have worn the Maple Leaf sweater during the team's 99 seasons, but you would have a difficult time finding three players who are more loved, or better represent the greatness of this franchise and its history, than Dave Keon, Turk Broda, and Tim Horton,"

This was the Leafs' centennial season and many events were planned, including the outdoor game and the great reveal of the Top 100 Maple Leafs. What better time for the former captain and Conn Smythe Trophy winner to return and be a part of this historic milestone.

On October 13, 2016, David Keon and several proud family members, along with representatives of Turk Broda and Tim Horton, were present for the unveiling of their statues. Finally, one of Toronto's most popular athletes has returned home.

The next day, the Top 100 Maple Leafs were announced at Real Sports Bar & Grill across from Scotiabank Arena and steps from "Legends Row," where the statues are displayed. Thirty-one Leaf historians, authors, and other media types were asked to rank the greatest Leaf players from 1 to 100. To no one's surprise, Dave Keon was voted as the best Toronto Maple Leaf of all time. Hall of Fame centres Syl Apps and Teeder Kennedy finished second and third. Curiously, James Van Riemsdyk was named 100th on the list. Its not that JVR wasn't a good player, but he had only been with the team for four years and was still active.

On October 15, prior to the Leafs' home opener, to the astonishment of all in attendance, the Leafs not only honoured Dave Keon's No. 14, but actually retired the number. And then all of the

Left to Right: Dick Duff, Jim Gregory, Johnny Bower, Dave Keon, Peter Ing, Stewart Gavin, Ric Nattress, and Kevin Maguire. (Photo by Lora Evans / Hat Trik Event Coverage)

previously honoured sweaters hanging in the rafters were lowered and new banners lifted with those numbers never to be worn by any Maple Leaf player again. The numbers—1, 4, 7, 9, 10, and 27—had not been used for years, and only No. 21 was still in use. That was JVR's number, and he switched to No. 25 that night. Of course, the ceremony was kept secret and only a few, including JVR, were notified about the happenings that night. The Leaf organization had changed their philosophy!

If finally retiring the sweater numbers was the only way to bring Dave Keon back, so be it. But Dave's stance was not just for himself but for all the other players whose numbers were just honoured. You can bet that Johnny Bower, Frank Mahovlich, Darryl Sittler, and the others previously honoured were pleased as well.

100 Top 100 Maple Leafs of All Time

As part of the Toronto Maple Leafs' centennial celebrations, 30 prominent hockey personalities plus a fan vote ranked the top 100 players from the St. Pats to the present. Of the 949 eligible players, 191 received at least one vote. 10 players had at least one first-place vote.

Top 100

1. Dave Keon
2. Syl Apps
3. Ted Kennedy
4. Darryl Sittler
5. Mats Sundin
6. Tim Horton
7. Johnny Bower
8. Borje Salming
9. Frank Mahovlich
10. Turk Broda
11. Charlie Conacher
12. George Armstrong

13. Doug Gilmour	46. Sweeney Schriner
14. Red Kelly	47. Harry Lumley
15. Wendel Clark	48. Phil Kessel
16. Busher Jackson	49. Babe Pratt
17. Hap Day	50. Bob Davidson
18. King Clancy	51. Lorne Chabot
19. Lanny McDonald	52. Tiger Williams
20. Rick Vaive	53. Gary Leeman
21. Max Bentley	54. Steve Thomas
22. Joe Primeau	55. Reg Noble
23. Allan Stanley	56. Gus Mortson
24. Ron Ellis	57. Ron Stewart
25. Ace Bailey	58. Mike Palmateer
26. Bob Pulford	59. Billy Harris
27. Red Horner	60. Gary Roberts
28. Dick Duff	61. Vincent Damphousse
29. Gord Drillon	62. John Anderson
30. Bob Baun	63. Bryan McCabe
31. Babe Dye	64. Bob Nevin
32. Carl Brewer	65. Howie Meeker
33. Sid Smith	66. Wally Stanowski
34. Norm Ullman	67. Gaye Stewart
35. Curtis Joseph	68. Eddie Shack
36. Bill Barilko	69. Nick Metz
37. Tomas Kaberle	70. Darcy Tucker
38. Tod Sloan	71. Ed Belfour
39. Harry Watson	72. Lorne Carr
40. Jimmy Thomson	73. Errol Thompson
41. Dave Andreychuk	74. Bill Ezinicki
42. Ian Turnbull	75. Bill Derlago
43. Terry Sawchuk	76. Bert Olmstead
44. Paul Henderson	77. Harry Cameron
45. Felix Potvin	78. Al Iafrate

79.	Ed Olczyk	90.	Jack Adams
80.	Jim McKenny	91.	Gus Bodnar
81.	George Hainsworth	92.	Cal Gardner
82.	Marcel Pronovost	93.	Tie Domi
83.	Alex Mogilny	94.	Brian Glennie
84.	Todd Gill	95.	Corb Denneny
85.	Mike Walton	96.	Larry Hillman
86.	Dave Ellett	97.	Wilf Paiement
87.	Baldy Cotton	98.	Russ Courtnall
88.	Dion Phaneuf	99.	Joe Klukay
89.	Jim Pappin	100.	James van Riemsdyk

Selection Committee

Bob Stellick, Mike Ferriman, Damian Cox, Mark Askin, Paul Hendrick, Brian Papineau, Christine Simpson, Elliotte Friedman, Scott Morrison, Mike Wilson, Joe Bowen, Andrew Podnieks, William Watters, Paul Patskou, John Shannon, John Iaboni, Mike Leonetti, Frank Orr, Jimmy Holmstrom, Dave Hodge, Mike Zeisberger, Bob Cole, Lance Hornby, Brian McFarlane, Kevin Shea, Mike Brophy, Pat Park, Gord Stellick, Howard Berger, plus the fan vote.

Acknowledgments

The author would like to thank Triumph Books for allowing him to write about his favourite subjects—hockey and the Toronto Maple Leafs. Special thanks go to Tom Bast, Adam Motin, and Jesse Jordan at Triumph, who were very kind and patient while listening to my pleas for a book and then editing my words. This book would not have been possible without co-author Paul Patskou who provided text, materials and reviewed every item that appears in this book. Paul is without question one of the leading authorities on Maple Leaf history. I would also like to thank my wife, Maria, and my son, David, for understanding how much I love to write about hockey and in particular the Maple Leafs.

Bibliography

Books

Batten, Jack. *Hockey Dynasty.* Pagurian Press, Toronto, 1969.

Batten, Jack. *The Leafs in Autumn.* MacMillan of Canada, Toronto, 1975.

Batten, Jack. *An Anecdotal History of the Toronto Maple Leafs.* Key Porter Books, Toronto, 1994

Baun, Bob. *Lowering the Boom—The Bobby Baun Story.* Stoddart Publishing, Toronto, 2000.

Berger, Howard. *Maple Leaf Moments.* Warwick Publishing, Toronto, 1994.

Bower, Johnny and Duff, Bob. *The China Wall—The Timeless Legend of Johnny Bower.* Fenn Publishing, Toronto, 2008.

Conacher, Brian. *As the Puck Turns.* John Wiley and Sons, Mississauga (Ontario), 2007.

Diamond, Dan. *Maple Leaf Magic.* Thorn Press, Don Mills, Ontario, 1993.

Ellis Ron and Shea Kevin. *Over the Boards: The Ron Ellis Story.* Fenn Publishing, Bolton, 2002.

Fitkin, Ed. *Come On Teeder!—The Story of Ted Kennedy.* Baxter Publishing Company, Toronto, 1950.

Fitkin, Ed. *Turk Broda of the Leafs.* Baxter Publishing Company, Toronto, 1950.

Henderson, Paul and Leonetti, Mike. *Shooting for Glory—The Paul Henderson Story.* Stoddart Publishing 1992.

Hewitt, Foster. *Hockey Night in Canada—The Story of the Toronto Maple Leafs.* Ryerson Press, Toronto, 1962.

Harris, Billy. *The Glory Years: Memories of a Decade 1955–1965*, Prentice-Hall, Toronto, 1989.

Houston, Bill. *Inside Maple Leaf Gardens: The Rise and Fall of the Toronto Maple Leafs.* McGraw-Hill Ryerson, 1989.

Hunt, Jim. *The Men in the Nets.* Ryerson Press, Toronto, 1967.

Imlach, Punch and Young, Scott. *Hockey is a Battle*, Macmillan of Canada, Toronto, 1969.

Leonetti, Mike. *Cold War: A Decade of Hockey's Greatest Rivalry 1959–1969.* Harper-Collins, 2001.

Leonetti, Mike. *Defining Moments.* Red Deer Press, Richmond Hill (Ontario), 2011.

Leonetti, Mike and Iaboni, John. *The Top 100 Maple Leafs of All Time.* Raincoast Books, Vancouver, 2007.

Leonetti, Mike. *Hockey Now!* (4th, 5th, 6th and 7th Editions), Firefly Books, Richmond Hill, Ontario, 2010.

Mahovlich, Ted. *The Big M.* Macmillan of Canada, Toronto, 1999.

McDonald, Lanny and Simmons, Steve. *Lanny.* McGraw-Hill Ryerson, Toronto, 1987.

Obodiac, Stan. *The Leafs: The First Fifty Years.* McClelland and Stewart, Toronto, 1976.

Obodiac, Stan. *Red Kelly.* Clarke, Irwin and Co., Toronto, 1971.

Parent, Bernie. *Bernie! Bernie! Bernie!* Prentice-Hall, Englewood Cliffs, New Jersey, 1975.

Salming, Borje and Karlsson, Gerhard. *Blood, Sweat and Hockey.* Harper-Collins, Toronto, 1991.

Shea, Kevin, *Without a Trace: The Bill Barilko Story.* Fenn Publishing, Bolton (Ontario), 2004.

Shea, Kevin and Patskou, Paul. *Diary of a Dynasty –Toronto Maple Leafs 1957–1967.* Firefly Books, Richmond Hill, 2010.

Sittler, Darryl and Goyens, Chrys. *Sittler.* Macmillan, Toronto, 1991.

Smythe, Conn and Young, Scott. *If You Can't Beat Them in the Alley,* McClelland and Stewart, Toronto, 1981.

Ulmer, Michael. *Captains: Nine Great Toronto Maple Leaf.* Macmillan of Canada, Toronto, 1995.

Williams, David and Lawton . James. *Tiger: A Hockey Story.* Harper-Collins, Toronto, 1986.

Newspapers
Globe and Mail
National Post
The Toronto Star
The Toronto Sun

Websites
cbcsports.ca
Hockey Hall of Fame.com
Mapleleafs.com
NHL.com
The Hockey News
SI.com
Wikipedia
Youtube.com

Media Guides
All Toronto Maple Leaf media guides issued since 1962

Game Programs
Toronto Maple Leaf game programs from the 1930s to 2013–14

Magazines
Hockey Illustrated (various issues)
Hockey Night in Toronto (various issues)
Hockey Pictorial (various issues)
Hockey World (various issues)
The Hockey News (various issues since 1947)
Sports Illustrated (various issues)

Guides and Record Books
NHL Guide & Record Book (various issues)
Total Hockey (2nd edition)
Total NHL
Total Stanley Cup (Playoff Guide)

Radio
FAN590 (in Toronto)
TSN 1050 (in Toronto)

Television
Hockey Night in Canada on CBC
That's Hockey on TSN
The NHL on TSN
The NHL on Sportsnet
Leafs TV
How I Met Your Mother
Cheers
The Wayne and Shuster Show
SCTV

Toronto game ticket featuring Maple Leafs superfan Tom Gaston.
(Author Collection)